·

THE LATE ROMAN ARMY

BY

GABRIELE ESPOSITO

ILLUSTRATED BY

GIUSEPPE RAVA

Cover image by Giuseppe Rava
Edited by Vincent W. Rospond
Winged Hussar Publishing, LLC, 1525 Hulse Road, Unit 1, Point Pleasant, NJ 08742

This edition published in 2016 Copyright ©Winged Hussar Publishing, LLC

ISBN 978-09963657-9-6
LCN 2016938428
Bibliographical references and index
1.Roman Army. 2. Ancient. 3. Military

For more information on Winged Hussar Publishing, LLC, visit us at:
https://www.WingedHussarPublishing.com

All illustrations are copyright of Giuseppe Rava

Preface

This book is dedicated to my parents, Maria Rosaria and Benedetto, for their continued efforts to help me in every moment of life and for their immense love. Someone said: "The only people who truly know your story, are the ones who help you write it"; that is particularly true for my parents, persons and teachers of precious humanity.

The initial idea behind this book came from my great friend Giuseppe Rava, whose illustrations and color plates make this work a real piece of art. Alexander Dumas said: "Friendship consists in forgetting what one gives and remembering what one receives"; however, as a true friend, I will never forget the opportunities that Giuseppe gave me and his innate generosity. His vivid style and perfect rendering of details have transformed a beautiful idea into an astonishing reality.

Special thanks are due to the excellent editor of this volume, Vincent Rospond. Sometimes you feel to be on the same wavelength with a person since the first talk: this was exactly the case of Vincent and I, in a morning of summer. I hope that the new projects with Winged Hussar Publishing which start with this book will continue to grow for many years to come, leading to the publication of many other interesting volumes like this. It is very difficult to find intelligent editors interested in military history, but when this happens the future results can only be very positive.

Very special thanks go to François Gilbert, for giving me permission to use his fantastic drawings of the Notitia Dignitatum's shield emblems. Without his generosity this book wouldn't have the magnificent section with all the shields from the Notitia in color. François is a great reenactor of ancient Rome's military and his books published by Éditions Errance are a must for all the lovers of this period of military history.

Another generous friend who contributed to the creation of this book is Richard Abels, professor of History at the United States Naval Academy. Much of the info contained in the sections "The organization of the late Roman Army" and "The ascendancy of the barbarians" is taken from his brilliant researches on this historical period. These are recollected on a fantastic website, which is an invaluable secondary source on the late Roman military:

http://www.usna.edu/Users/history/abels/hh381/late_roman_barbarian_militaries.htm

Last but not least, credit should go to Luke Ueda-Sarson for his astonishing website on the Notitia Dignitatum; this is the best single source available on this precious ancient text and was thus extensively used by me to find information on the single military units listed in the Notitia. Everyone interested in the Notitia Dignitatum should visit this fantastic resource:

http://lukeuedasarson.com/NotitiaPatterns.html

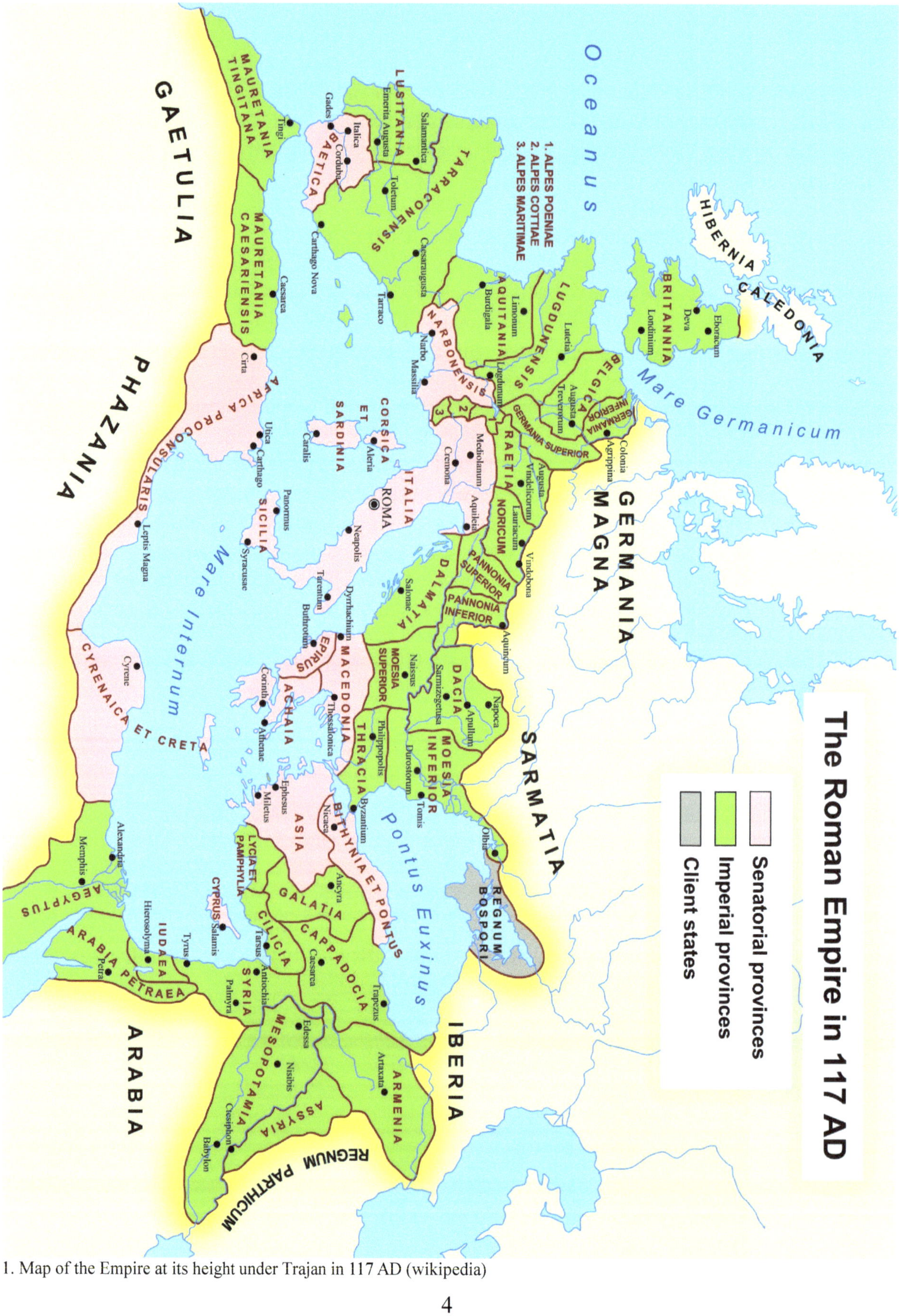

Fig 1. Map of the Empire at its height under Trajan in 117 AD (wikipedia)

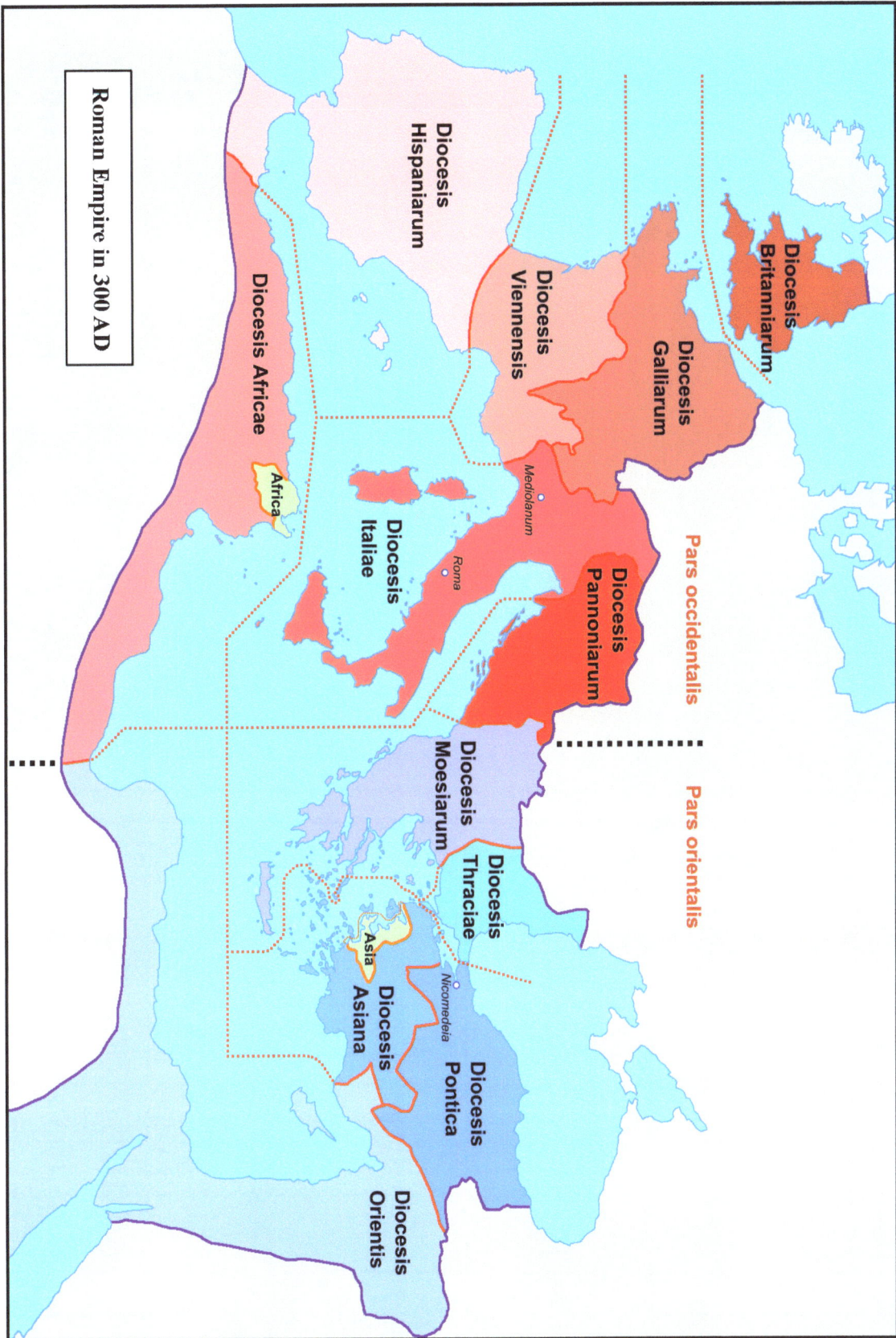

Fig 2. Map of the Roman Empire in 300 AD (wikipedia)

Roman Empire in 300 AD

Diocesis Hispaniarum

Diocesis Viennensis

Diocesis Galliarum

Diocesis Britanniarum

Diocesis Africae

Africa

Diocesis Italiae

Mediolanum

Roma

Diocesis Pannoniarum

Pars occidentalis

Pars orientalis

Diocesis Moesiarum

Diocesis Thraciae

Asia

Diocesis Asiana

Nicomedeia

Diocesis Pontica

Diocesis Orientis

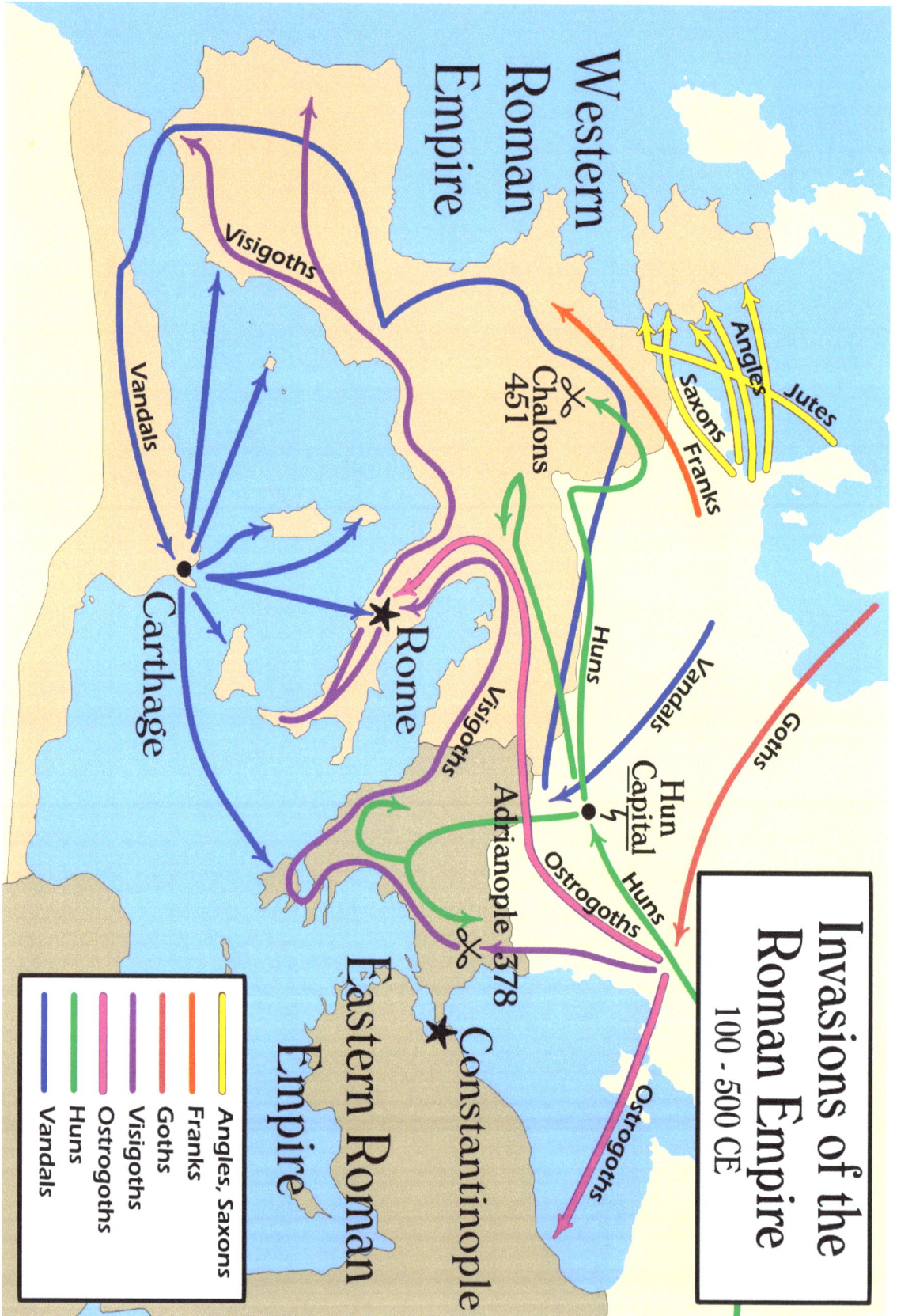

Fig 3. The invasion of the Barbarians (wikipedia)

Introduction

For purposes of being tidy, many historians designate the late Roman Empire from the accession of the Emperor Diocletian in year 284 to 476 A.D., with the deposition of the last western Roman Emperor Romulus Augustus (Romulus Augustulus). That said, this designation should be viewed loosely. Some aspects of the organization of the army as of 284 were in existence prior to that date and others continued to exist after the fall of the western Empire in the armies of the Germanic kingdoms or in the eastern part of the Roman Empire. One of the issues faced in untangling the history and organization of this era is the continued use of terms throughout the period that can sometimes mean different things in different eras.

The armed forces of the western Empire continued as a viable force during the years 395-476 when they were properly led, but the revolving rulers of the western Empire were not better organized to utilize their forces in response to changing internal and external politics. The eastern Empire, however, remained largely intact in structure and size until the reign of the great Emperor Justinian I (527-565). Many traditional historians have portrayed the later army as inferior because it was not using the same organization as under Principate or "the good Emperors." For a long time the army of this era has been widely regarded as a motley collection of badly trained and poorly equipped peasant farmers, increasingly augmented by "barbarian" soldiers (foederati or mercenaries, mostly of Germanic origins) who diluted the proud Roman forces.

This negative image of the late Roman soldiers seems to be reinforced by the fact that the western Empire was overrun and occupied by the Germanic tribes. The idea that the late Roman forces were inferior was first espoused when Europe rediscovered Roman history during the Renaissance and repeated as fact continuing up to the 19th century. There are many factors that contributed in the fall of the western Empire, but in this book will try to explain how the late Roman army was still functional to the military needs of the Empire and why the traditional idea that we have of it is wrong and mostly outdated.

The general picture of the late Roman military has been completely changed by the studies and researches of the last three decades, which have clearly demonstrated that an evaluation of the late Roman military forces is not as simple as been portrayed for so long. The Roman army of the fourth century may have been very different from that of the Julio-Claudians in many respects but this difference does not necessarily imply decline. The Roman society of the first century was not intrinsically better than that of the fourth century and the later Roman army was just as effective in pursuing the defensive goals for which it was designed as its earlier counterpart was in fulfilling Rome's expansionist mission during the early decades of the Empire.

The long evolution of the Roman military forces up to this period was predicated on the fact that the early Imperial army had proved incapable of dealing with the new threats to the Empire, which emerged during the later centuries as mass migration of tribes was more and more common. When the army kept on the offensive, it fulfilled the needs of the Empire at the time. As the financial fortunes declined, the primary mission of the army was shifted to a defensive one, to which commanders adapted their tactical doctrine. Had the system not adapted to change, the Empire would surely have fallen considerably earlier than it actually did. Obviously, because of its defensive nature, the later army has no chance to compare very favorably with the expansionist force of the earlier days: in history, defensive armies never seem to hold much interest and admiration. In addition to this, the appearance of the late Roman soldiers has much more in common with the Norman knights on the Bayeux tapestry than with the legionaries wearing the lorica segmentata on Trajan's column.

THE LATE ROMAN ARMY

Weaponry, as well as organization and tactics, had been progressively adapted to the new needs of a changing political organism, which was coming under strong pressures from the inside as well as from the bordering populations. Luckily we have a certain number of good primary sources, which enable us to create a quite complete and interesting reconstruction of the late Roman soldiers. Much of our evidence for the deployment and organization of the late Roman military units is contained in a single, and thus fundamental, document: the *Notitia Dignitatum*. Much of the material included in this book has been taken from this fantastic primary source and, for this reason, a section of this work will be entirely devoted to it. One of the main literary sources for the 4th-century army is the *Res Gestae* of Ammianus Marcellinus, whose surviving books cover the years 353-378. Marcellinus, who was a veteran soldier, is generally regarded as a reliable and valuable writer; however, he is rarely specific regarding army's strength and units in existence in his time. The third major source for the late Roman army is the body of laws published in the Theodosian Code (438 AD), which contains numerous Imperial decrees relating to all aspects of the army's regulation and administration.

An interesting, albeit unreliable source of tactics and organization, is the treatise *De re militari* written by Vegetius in the late 4th or early 5th-century. It contains considerable information on the late army, but spends a great deal of space exalting the military forces of the Republic and Principate against the then modern forces. Vegetius' statements, however, seem to indicate a lack of practical military experience. What little we do know about the author indicates he was a lower level administrator and where what he says can be corroborated he is useful.

Some scholars of this period have complained that there is a dearth of material, especially if compared with those available for the early Empire. In addition, official stamps of military units on building materials were much rarer. This negative trend should not be seen as a factor indicating a decline in the Roman army's administrative sophistication: papyrus sources from Egypt show that military units continued to keep detailed written records up to and during the 4th century. Most likely, the quantitative decline in inscriptions could be explained as the result of a changing fashion, in part influenced by the increase of barbarian recruits in the army and the rise of Christianity.

Fig 4. SPQR (wikipedia)

Chronology of Major Political and Military Events 284 - 476 A.D.

284   Diocletian, son of a Dalmatian slave, becomes Emperor and rules the eastern part of the Empire from Nicomedia.

285   Diocletian, after proclaiming himself the human manifestation of Jupiter, reunites the Empire and ends 50 years of civil war.

286   Diocletian appoints Maximian to rule the west, with capital in Milan.

293   Diocletian institutes the mechanism of the "tetrarchy", according to which each Emperor chooses his successor ahead of time. Diocletian chooses Galerius, while Maximian chooses Constantius Chlorus.

295   The Sassanids invade the eastern Empire again.

299   The Sassanids surrender to Galerius, who annexes Armenia, Georgia and Upper Mesopotamia to the Empire.

303   Diocletian and Maximian order a general persecution of the Christians, including the destruction of all churches and burning of all Christian books.

305   Diocletian and Maximian abdicate in favor of Galerius and Constantius, but civil war erupts again.

306   Constantius dies: his son Flavius Valerius Constantinus (Constantine) is acclaimed by his troops as new vice-Emperor of Galerius. The Praetorian Guard appoints Maximian's son Maxentius Emperor, instead of Galerius' choice Severus.

308   Galerius appoints another Emperor, Licinius.

311   Galerius dies, leaving Maxentius and Constantine to fight for the throne of the western Empire.

312   Constantine defeats Maxentius, thus becoming Emperor of the west, and disbands the Praetorian Guard.

313   Constantine's ally Licinius defeats Maxentius' ally Maximinus and becomes co-Emperor in the east. Constantine ends the persecutions of the Christians with the Edict of Milan.

314   Constantine defeats Licinius and obtains control over all Roman Europe except Thracia, while Licinius keeps Africa and Asia.

323   Constantine defeats decisively Licinius and becomes the sole Roman Emperor.

324   Constantine I founds a new city, Constantinople (Byzantium).

330   Constantine I moves the capital of the Roman Empire to Constantinople.

337   Constantine dies and his sons split the Empire: Constantine II (Spain, Britain and Gaul), Constans I (Italy, Africa, Macedonia and Greece) and Constantius II (eastern provinces).

338   Constans, unhappy with the division of power, petitions his brothers to redivide the Empire.

350   In a military revolt led by the usurper Magnentius, Constans is murdered by his own troops at the age of 27.

353   Constantius II defeats the usurper Magnentius in battle and becomes sole Emperor.

360   Pagan general Julian (the "apostate") defeats an invasion of barbarians and is declared Emperor by his Germanic troops.

363   Julian dies while attempting to invade the Sassanid Empire, which recaptures Nisibis and Armenia. General Valentinian becomes the new Emperor.

364   Valentinian delegates Valens as Emperor of the east.

376   Fleeing Hunnic aggression, the Goths under the leadership of Fritigern cross the Danube and enter the eastern Empire as political refugees.

377   Following harsh treatment by the Romans, the Goths revolt. Beginning of the Gothic War.

378   The Visigoths defeat the Romans at the battle of Adrianople.

380   Theodosius I proclaims Christianity as the sole religion of the Roman Empire. The Visigoths defeat the Roman army in Macedonia.

382   The Goths and the Empire conclude a peace treaty, according to which the former are allowed to settle along the southern Danube frontier (in the province of Thrace) and are granted significant self-governance.

383   Theodosius splits the Empire in two parts (east and west), which are granted to his infant sons Arcadius and Honorius. Civil war erupts against the western usurper Magnus Maximus.

387   Theodosius defeats Magnus Maximus.

392   Theodosius fights a civil war against the western usurper Eugenius.

393   Theodosius forbids the Olympic Games and shuts down the temple of Zeus at Olympia.

394   Theodosius defeats Eugenius at the battle of the Frigidus.

395   Theodosius dies and the Empire is divided in a definitive way. Milan is capital of the western half, Constantinople is capital of the eastern one. The two parts of the Empire are granted to Theodosius' minor sons Arcadius and Honorius, but ruled by their advisors Rufinus and Flavius Stilicho. Alaric unifies the Visigoths in the Balkans and invades Greece.

397   Stilicho attacks Alaric, but is not able to defeat him in a definitive way. The eastern Emperor signs a deal with the Visigoths.

398   Stilicho puts down the Gildonic revolt in Africa.

401   Alaric invades Italy, but is defeated by Stilicho.

402   The western Roman Empire moves the capital from Milan to Ravenna.

405   Radagaisus leads a Gothic raid into Italy.

406   Radagaisus is captured and executed. Vandals and Alans invade France after crossing the Rhine.

407   Stilicho (of Vandal descent) stops the Vandals on their way to Italy.

408   Stilicho is deposed.

409   Vandals and Alans invade Spain.

410   The Visigoths sack Rome. The last Roman legions withdraw from England.

418   The Emperor grants Visigoths the right to settle in Aquitaine, in return for their military support against Vandals and Alans.

425   The eastern Emperor Theodosius II installs Valentinian III as Emperor of the west.

427   Gensenric's Vandals cross the strait of Gibraltar and land in north Africa.

430   The Roman Empire signs a first peace treaty with the Huns.

435   The Roman Empire signs a second peace treaty with the Huns.

439   The Vandals capture Carthage.

443   The Burgundians receive official permission to settle in Savoy.

450   Theodosius II dies and is succeeded by Marcian, the first Roman Emperor to be crowned by a religious leader (the patriarch of Constantinople).

451   Roman victory at the battle of the Catalaunian Plains.

452   The Huns, under command of Attila, invade Italy.

453   Death of Attila.

455   The Vandals sack Rome.

469   Attila's son Dengizich is captured and executed.

476   Odoacer, a leader of the Germanic mercenaries in the service of Rome, deposes the western Roman Emperor Romulus Augustulus and thereby terminates the western Roman Empire.

Fig 5. The late period of the Roman Empire was characterized by both civil wars and conflicts against external threats. From left to right: cataphract, legionary, Hun cavalryman and infantryman of the Romanenses (one of the pseudocomitatenses units under command of the magister equitum praesentalis in Gaul). The legionary has the traditional "Chi-Rho" emblem depicted on his shield, a very common device since the reign of Emperor Constantine. (Giuseppe Rava)

Fig 6. Diocletian (wikipedia)

Rebirth 284 – 361 AD

The ascension of Diocletian in 284 is generally marked as the end of the crisis of the third century. After a period of political upheaval within the Empire, an era of stability lasted for twenty years as Diocletian tried to reorganize the Empire to adapt to the changing situation. The Empire was divided into two administrative districts under two Augusti, supported by two Caesars. Diocletian faced several major issues upon his ascension to the purple. The first was an economic depression caused by incessant warfare, which led to depopulation and lack of production. The second was an army that needed to reorganize to meet the increased barbarian threats. Last, he felt the need to update the administrative organization of running the Empire.

Diocletian initially tried to redo the coinage, but eventually resorted to price freezes in 301 with the Edict of Prices. This did not better, but eventually an annual state budget was established based on the ability of each province to contribute. The economic reforms did not alleviate all the issues faced by local populations, as people moved from place to place to avoid some taxes. This practice resulted in additional edicts that tied people to the land of their birth.

The army abandoned its old static defense and adopted a new mobile one which resulted in the establishment of new types of troops: Limitanei (frontier troops) and Comitatenses (field army). This substitued the old idea of Legionaries and Auxiliaries and placed all soldiers on an equal footing.

The size of the Empire, combined with regular enemy pressure on the borders, required a change to the way the Empire should be administered. During the early Empire, the military and administration were under the same control. These duties were separated by Diocletian to create professional class administrators and soldiers. The Empire had two Augusti (East and West), each supported by a Caesar. The territory of the Empire was thus divided into four parts, each governed by a Praefectus, and subdivided into Dioceses, controlled by a Vicarii. Each Diocese was divided into Provinces under a Governor. Each

Fig 7. Roman soldiers battling the Persians(wikipedia)

provincial army was commanded by a Dux. While more flexible in controlling the Empire, the new organization greatly increased the bureaucracy, which augmented the cost of running the administration. When the Augustus retired, the Caesar was supposed to take over. This system lasted for a few years and then imploded.

Constantine was proclaimed Augustus by the army in Britain when his father died and quickly came into conflict with Maxentius: the new civil war was resolved by the battle of Milvian Bridge in 312, which resulted in a reunited Empire. Diocletian had moved the center of government east to Nicomedia, but in 326 Constantine founded the city of Constantinople. Constantine embraced Christianity, and by doing so was able to confiscate treasures in the pagan temples, which partly helped to prop up the economy. After the death of Constantine, the Empire was divided between his three sons; it was eventually reunited by Constantius during the period 340-361. The Empire remained relatively stable under Julian, until his death in 363; in that year the Empire was split again and the Emperors who followed were not strong enough to maintain power for any length of time. Slowly, controlled settlement of the Germanic tribes crossing the northern borders transformed into uncontrolled migration, with the result that the imperial administration lost the ability to maintain political and economic order.

Fig 8. A Dacian Draco standard as pictured on Trajan's column. This was eventually adopted by Roman forces.

The Ascendancy of the Barbarians, 350-378 A.D.

For the ancient Greeks and Romans the word "barbarian" was primarily used to mean "non-Greek" or "non-Roman" and, by extension, non-civilized. After the Edict of Caracalla in 212 the definition of "barbarians" became blurred as all free people of the Empire were considered citizens. As Germanic tribes were allowed to settle within the boundaries of the Empire and used in the army, the term "barbarian" is more loosely applied by modern historians. A Roman citizen of Germanic origins was to the Romans of the late Empire simply a Roman. Every population having a different culture from their own was considered as "barbarian" by the Romans: Germanic tribes like the Alemanni, Goths, Vandals, Burgundians, Franks, Suebi and Gepids; but also other peoples such as Picts, Sarmatians, Alans, Huns, Isaurians and Moors. From a military point of view, those lumped together as "the Germans" were the most important group. Until the battle of Adrianople in 378, the Empire was able to relatively contain Germanic incursions, the biggest issue faced during those years being internal threats. After Adrianople, the central authority of the western Roman Empire was partly replaced by tribal control of Germanic kings who had loosely pledged allegiance to Rome.

The German-speaking barbarian tribes, settling along the frontiers of the Rhine and Danube in the 4th and 5th centuries, were mainly composed of warriors/farmers. From a political point of view, they were organized into "cantons" (pagi) consisting of several villages, each having its own dominant family. The leading families of each village recognized the sovereign authority of a king or of a royal family. Rome's traditional policy of favouring and enriching Germanic client kings led, in the long run, to the emergence of larger and more cohesive tribal confederations, as stronger kings absorbed the cantons of weaker neighbours. Meanwhile, Roman trade progressively "romanized" culturally and economically the elite groups of the Germanic tribes. The barbarian cantons were militarized and violent societies: kings and nobles maintained strong military households, with many young retainers who served as their bodyguards and also as "professional" core of their armies in case of war. Due to the strong agrarian character of the Germanic economy and society, warfare was conducted as much as possible during agricultural down times, either during winter months or between the spring and autumn harvests.

From the time of Caesar Germanic warfare against the Romans tended to be small-scale, involving raids across the border made by the forces of individual cantons (numbering no more than a couple of thousand men). These expeditions were primarily made to acquire booty and not to conquer territories. Usually they were followed by punitive responses into German territory by Roman limitanei. Until 350 AD the western Roman Empire experienced intermittent incursions but most of these were contained after an initial foray. In the previous decade it had experienced a Frankish raid into Gaul and some unrest in Britain, but no serious threat to its stability. In the eastern half, war along the frontier with Persia had raged in the early 340s, as several border towns and fortresses changed hands, and continued sporadically until 353-358 AD, when the expansionist Shapur II had to turn his attention to his own eastern frontiers (which were attacked by nomad tribes).

In the west, peace was first shattered when the soldiers of the Comes Galliae revolted against Emperor Constans in 350 and proclaimed their commander Magnentius as Emperor. Constans fled upon learning of the revolt, but was captured and killed. Magnentius occupied Italy by force, while Spain and Africa peacefully submitted to his rule. At the same time another general, Vetranio, took advantage of the situation by assuming command of the Comes Illyrici. The eastern Emperor Constantius II, who was in Antioch monitoring a threatened invasion by the Persian Shapur II, eventually responded to these

Fig 9. Frankish warriors sacking a Roman villa in Gaul, during the period 350-357 AD. The Roman heavy cavalrymen facing them are from the Domestici equites of the western Empire. Most of them wear lorica hamata cuirasses and have a long cavalry spatha. Note the peculiar Germanic hair style of the Franks and their common use of the francisca (throwing axe). (Giuseppe Rava)

usurpations in late 350. He marched his army into the Balkans and cowed Vetranio into giving up his command. Constantius II then defeated Magnentius in a field battle in Pannonia, thus forcing the usurper to retreat into Italy.

A confederation of Franks and Alemanni took advantage of the general unrest to launch a raid into Gaul. Civil war raged until 353 AD, when Magnentius committed suicide in Gaul, after having lost Italy, Spain and Africa. In the wake of civil war, Gaul had been left vulnerable to barbarian attacks; for this reason, Constantius II appointed a veteran general of Frankish descent named Silvanus as Comes Galliae in 354, in order to counter Frankish incursions over the lower Rhine. The Emperor led his forces against the Alemanni across the upper Rhine meanwhile becoming suspicious of Silvanus when he payed the Franks to withdraw from Roman territory rather than attacking them. Fearing arrest and execution, Silvanus responded by declaring himself Emperor in the August of 355.

Constantius II then sent his magister equitum of the eastern Empire, Ursicinus, into Gaul in order to bribe some of Silvanus' troops and convince them to kill their master. The Franks in the north and the Alemanni in the south took advantage of this situation to invade Gaul again. Due to the emergency, Constantius II elevated his young cousin Julian to the rank of Caesar and sent him to Gaul to contain the Franks. Between 356 and 359 both Constantius II and Julian waged war along the Rhine limes against various Germanic tribes and confederations. Despite being outnumbered, Julian won a major victory over the Alemanni at Strasbourg in 357 AD. With Gaul for the moment safe, Julian was also able to send his magister militum per Gallias to Britain, in order to counter a series of major incursions by the Picts. In 359, Shapur II finally defeated the nomad tribes on his eastern frontiers and renewed his war against the eastern Empire.

Understanding the magnitude of the Persian threat, Constantius II summoned units from the western Empire to join him in the eastern campaign. Unwilling to leave Gaul, the troops responded by elevating Julian to the rank of Augustus (senior Emperor). Constantius II refused to ratify this promotion and Julian marched east against his cousin. A new civil war was avoided only thanks to the sudden death of Constantius II in 361. However, the Persian threat remained: as a result Julian attempted to protect the borders by organizing a major expedition against the Sassanids. Leading a large army of 65,000 men, he marched down the Euphrates and defeated the Persians at Ctesiphon. Julian was unable to take the city by siege and while there he learned that a Sassanid relief army was going to arrive, forcing his army to withdraw. The retreat soon became a fighting march, as the Persian Army caught up with the Romans. Julian died from a wound and the soldiers chose one of their generals, Jovian, as the new Emperor. Cut off from further retreat by a superior enemy force, Jovian was forced to accept a humiliating peace that

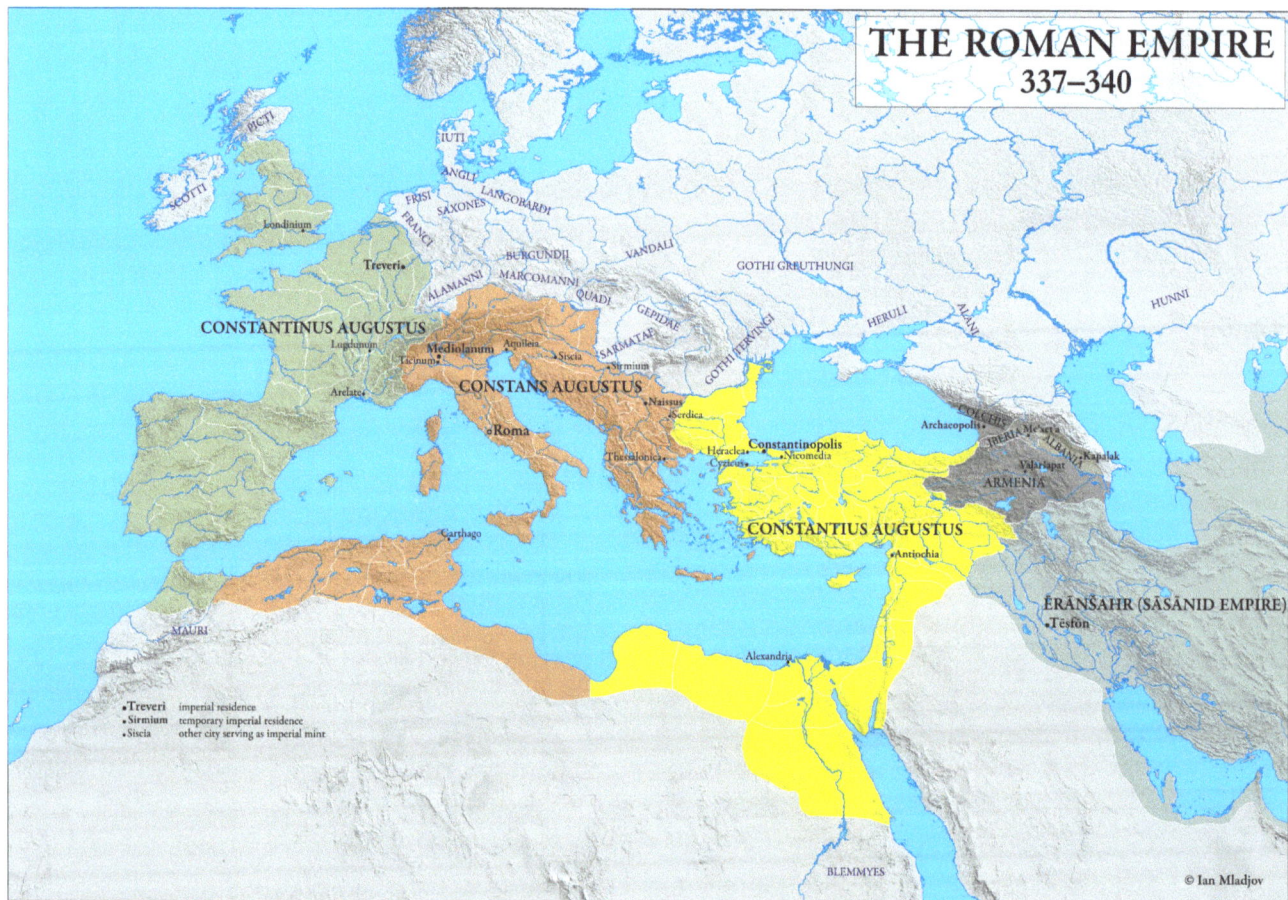

Fig 10. The Roman Empire in the Mid-4th Century (USNA)

included the surrender of all the Roman territories east of the Tigris. His death in 364 AD led the army to elect another professional soldier as Emperor, the successful military commander Valentinian I.

In turn, Valentinian chose his brother Valens as co-Emperor: Valentinian assumed command over the western half of the Empire and Valens over the eastern one. In 367-368 the two brothers had to face threats on all frontiers of the Empire. Valentinian sent troops to counter major barbarian incursions in Britain and another raid across the Rhine by the Alemanni. At the same time Valens began a war against the Goths of King Athanaric and forced them back against the Carpathians. In the same period the Sassanids captured the King of Armenia, a Roman ally, and invaded Georgia in 370; Valentinian found himself fighting enemies on all fronts. The Saxons began incursions into Gaul which forced him to stop them while at the same time putting down a rebellion. Valens then sent troops to support the Armenians against the Persians; this resulted in an Armenian victory over Shapur and a five year truce.

During the next three years the Romans found themselves fighting against Sarmatians and Quadi in the northwestern Balkans and putting down an Isaurian revolt in Asia. Valentinian died in 375 AD while planning a punitive expedition against the Quadi. The army immediately acclaimed his son Valentinian II as Emperor, with Valentinian's older brother Gratian assuming guardianship over the child and acting as co-Emperor.

In the early 370s, the arrival of the Huns into the plains of eastern Europe created a completely new strategic situation: in 376 they drove the Gothic Tervingi to seek refuge in the eastern Roman Empire. At that time the Roman border was quite permeable and it was not uncommon for Germanic tribes

Fig 11. Legionary of the Cortoriacenses and Gothic heavy cavalryman. The Cortoriacenses were one of the legiones comitatenses under command of the magister equitum praesentalis in Gaul. (Giuseppe Rava)

to settle within the Empire. What was unusual in 376 AD was the very high number of those who poured across the Danube. Emperor Valens' decision to enable the Goths' crossing of the Danube might not have proved so disastrous, if only the officials charged with supervising this operation had not provoked the starving Tervingi into pillaging the countryside. This, in turn, led to the battle of Adrianople between Valens and the Goths led by Fritigern.

On the morning of 9 August 378 AD, Emperor Valens left from Adrianople toward the location of the Gothic camp north of the city. At around 14:30, after marching for seven hours over difficult terrain, the Roman soldiers reached their objective in disorder, exhausted and dehydrated. The Gothic camp had been set up on the top of a hill. The Goths, except for their cavalry which was at a distance making use of better grazing grounds, took position in front of their wagon circle, which held their families and possessions. The surrounding fields were burnt to delay and harass the Romans with smoke, while negotiations took place for an exchange of hostages. Some Roman units began the battle without orders to do so, believing that they would have achieved an easy victory. The Romans attacked the circle of wagons but, lacking support and coordination, were easily repulsed. At that moment the Gothic cavalry, alerted by messengers from the embattled wagon circle, arrived to support the infantry. Their arrival changed the tactical situation, because the Roman cavalry was no match for the heavily equipped Gothic horsemen.

Fig 12. View of the Battle of Adrianople (9 August 378) from the Roman side. Note the "draco" standard on the right and the plumbatae carried on the back of the shields. (Giuseppe Rava)

As a result, the Roman horse was simply swept off the field. The Gothic infantry saw the tide turning and abandoned its defensive positions, beginning to advance against the Romans. In the past a Roman infantry force of this size (including 7 legions, more or less 7,000 heavy infantrymen) would have been able to hold the ground or retire in good order: instead, for the first time in a major contest fought by the Romans, a heavy cavalry force proved itself the complete master of the Roman heavy infantry. Attacked from all sides and under the terrible impacts of the devastating Gothic cavalry charges, the Roman troops fell into disarray and collapsed. In the rout, the Emperor was abandoned by his guards; Valens' final fate is unknown, but he probably died anonymously on the field. The immediate upshot of the battle was that Valens' successor, Emperor Theodosius I, found it necessary to contract a treaty with the Goths, which allowed them to settle within the Empire under their own rulers and laws, in return for providing troops when called upon to do so.

Fig 13. Emperor Valens fleeing from the battlefield of Adrianople. He wears a richly decorated tunic and cloak (with clavii and orbiculi), plus a pileus pannonicus covered with fur. The soldiers escorting the Emperor are from the Schola scutariorum secunda and Lanciarii seniores. The Lanciarii seniores were one of the legiones palatinae under command of the magister militum praesentalis I in the eastern Empire. The heavy cavalrymen of the Scholae Palatinae have lorica hamata or lorica squamata cuirasses, while the officer of the Lanciarii seniores on the left wears a leather muscle cuirass. Note the various models of helmet used, in particular that of the cavalryman on the right (which is very similar to contemporary "sports helmets").(Giuseppe Rava)

Fig 14. Scene from the Vandal Sack of Rome (455 AD), showing the capture of Licinia Eudoxia and of her daughter Eudocia. During the 440s, King Genseric and Emperor Valentinian III had betrothed their children, Huneric and Eudocia, to strengthen the alliance between Romans and Vandals reached with a peace treaty in 442. In 455 Valentinian was killed by the usurper Petronius Maximus, who rose to the throne and married Valentinian's widow Licinia Eudoxia. In addition, he had his son Palladius marry Eudocia: this move, however, damaged Genseric's ambitions. The King of the Vandals thus claimed that the broken betrothal was an invalidation of his peace treaty with Valentinian and set sail to attack Rome. Upon the Vandal arrival, Pope Leo I implored Genseric to abstain from murder and destruction of the city by fire. Genseric agreed and the gates of Rome were thrown open to him and his warriors. The Vandals looted great amounts of treasure from the city and also took Licinia Eudoxia and her daughters as hostages. Eudocia later married Huneric as planned. (Giuseppe Rava)

The Bagaudae

The Bagaudae was a term applied to groups of peasant insurgents who revolted against the Empire during the Third Century Crisis; however this phenomenon did not end in the third century, but persisted until the end of the western Empire. There is little primary information available about the origins of the Bagaudae and their impact on the structures of the Empire; what we know for sure is that they were particularly active in the areas of Gaul and Spain where the groups of insurgents were strong and numerous.

The name "Bagaudae" probably meant "fighters"; in fact, they were considered by the Imperial authorities as brigands who roamed the countryside looting and pillaging. While their origins may not be clear, the majority of them seem to have been impoverished local free peasants, who were later reinforced by brigands, runaway slaves and deserters from the army. The main aim of these peasants was to resist the ruthless labor exploitation of the late Roman proto-feudal manorial system and the punitive laws common in this area of the Empire. The invasions, military anarchy and disorders of the third century had caused an ongoing degradation of the regional power structure of the Empire; for this reason the Bagaudae were able to achieve some temporary and scattered successes, thanks to the local leadership of members of the underclass as well as former members of local ruling elites.

After the Bagaudae came to full attention of the central authorities around AD 284, re-establishment of the social order was swift and severe. In 286 the Caesar Maximian, under the aegis of the Emperor Diocletian, crushed the most important bands of Bagaudae which were active in Gaul. These were led by two leaders, known as Amandus and Aelianus. They were most likely members of the local Gallo-Roman landowning class, who then became "tyrants" (i.e. chiefs of the Bagaudae) and rebelled against the grinding taxation, garnishment of their lands, harvests and manpower by the predatory agents of the late Roman Empire (the "frumentarii publicani").

The "Panegyric of Maximian", dating to AD 289 and attributed to Claudius Mamertinus, relates that during the Bagaudae uprisings of 284–285 in southern Gaul: "simple farmers sought military garb; the plowman imitated the infantryman, the shepherd the cavalryman, the rustic harvester of his own crops the barbarian enemy". While they were technically Imperial farmers and citizens, the Bagaudae were essentially marauding rogues. The social phenomenon of the Bagaudae did not end with the repressions following the Third Century Crisis. The Bagaudae revolted again in the mid-fourth century, during the reign of Constantius, in conjunction with the invasion of Gaul by the Alemanni. Around 360, the historian Aurelius Victor noted attacks of the Bagaudae in the peripheries of the larger towns and walled cities.

In the fifth century Bagaudae revolts occurred in the Loire valley and Brittany, around 409-17, with the peasants battling armies sent against them by Flavius Aetius. There are indications that he used "foederati" such as the Alans under their King Goar to suppress a revolt of the Bagaudae in Armorica. During the same period, the Bagaudae are also mentioned in the province of Macedonia, the only time they emerged in the eastern Empire (which may be due to the economic hardships suffered under Emperor Arcadius). By the middle of the fifth century they are mentioned in control of large parts of central Gaul and the Ebro valley in Spain. In Hispania, King Rechiar of the Suevi allied himself with the local Bagaudae, in order to ravage the remaining Roman settlements on his territory (it was the only case of an alliance between a Germanic ruler and a band of rebel peasants).

While the depredations of the ruling classes were mostly responsible for the uprisings of the Bagaudae, the fifth-century writer Salvian, in the treatise "De gubernatione Dei", noted that the misery of the Roman world was all due to the neglect of God's commandments and the terrible sins of every class of society. It was not simply that slaves and servants were thieves and runaways, wine-bibbers and gluttons: the upper classes were much worse. According to Salvian, it was the harshness and greed that drove the poor to join the Bagaudae and flee for shelter to the barbarian invaders. With the final collapse of the Roman authority in the western Empire and the rise of the successor Germanic kingdoms, the Bagaudae begin to slowly disappear from recorded history.

Fig 15. Cavalryman of the Bagaudae. He has very light equipment, being armed only with a verutum and spatha. The wicker shield that he carries is very simple and easy to produce. The tunic is a Roman military one (with clavii and orbiculi), while the cloak and trousers clearly show Celtic influence. (Giuseppe Rava)

Fig 16. Bagaudae looting a Roman city in Gaul. Two of the brigands are probably ex-soldiers, because they wear military tunics. The figure on the left has even a shield, which identifies him as a deserter from the Sagittarii Nervii Gallicani (one of the auxilia palatina units under command of the magister equitum praesentalis in Gaul). The striped trousers of the same figure are clearly a Celtic item of dress. Note that the bandit on the right is stealing a couple of Celtic "torcs".(Giuseppe Rava)

Fig 17. Bagaudae ambushing Roman soldiers of the Cornuti seniores (who were one of the auxilia palatina units under command of the magister peditum praesentalis in Italy). The bandits of this group seem to be very well equipped and, probably, are all deserters (one has even a lorica hamata). On the left you can see what seems to be an "officer", wearing leather muscle cuirass with pteruges. The archers have wooden longbows. (Giuseppe Rava)

The Final Years 385-500

The traditional history of the late Roman period says that the influx of barbarians in the army and the rise of Christianity led to the fall of the Empire. This is an oversimplification of the issue that ignores many components of the late Roman period. The influx of the Goths escaping the pressures of the Huns in the later part of the 4th Century combined with inept Emperors and military rivalries in the army all conspired to drag the Empire down as a whole, but the west in particular.

Theodosius the Great stepped into the void during 379-392, but was able to unite both east and west into one force; his successors, however, were not up to the task ahead of them. There were additional raids into Gaul which de-populated the provinces and added to the financial and manpower woes. When the Gothic peoples were finally settled in the borders of the Empire, in many cases the regular administration was never fully reestablished and rather than integrating the people into the Empire, they remained with their own political and military organizations. The common theme of the later period is civil wars which depopulated a great deal of the Empire. Because of the limited tax base, the Emperors were pressed to pay for the administration of government and the military, which opened the door for generals to promise troops pay to follow them.

When the Germanic peoples started to settle inside the borders of the Empire, in many cases the regular administration was never fully reestablished; rather than being integrated into the Empire, the barbarian peoples remained with their own political and military organizations. Another common element of the later period was civil wars, which led to an intensification of the depopulation. Because of the limited tax base, the last Emperors were pressed to pay for the administration of the government and military, something which caused widespread corruption and the political ascendancy of generals who could buy the loyalty of mercenary troops.

In the early 5th Century the ethnic Vandal general Stilicho rose to prominence in the western part of the Empire and faced one emergency after another. He was forced to accept any and all troops into his forces which meant that they had little or no experience or discipline to speak of. This situation was exacerbated by raids of nominal allies such as the Goths, which destroyed the infrastructure, populace and the ability to feed troops of the Empire.

A series of events then hastened the decline of the Empire. By 405-6 the next huge wave of

Fig 18. Stilicho from the Monza Cathedral, 395 AD

tribes escaping the Huns entered Gaul without major opposition. In 409 Constantine III rebelled against the Emperor and took the troops from Britain to Gaul, leaving the Britons to their own defense. Alaric sacked Rome in 410 and the Diocese of Africa seceded from the western Empire to enter the eastern one, refusing to send grain to Rome, and thus creating a major food shortage. As early as 418 the Vandals and Alans had occupied Hispania. During this period there were several efforts to replace the Eastern or Western Emperor in order to unite the Empire once more, but this only helped to weaken both parts, especially the western one.

By the late 430's parts of Hispania, southern Gaul and Armorica had been lost to the invaders and the Rhine frontier was no longer stable, which meant the border was open to more incursions. In 429 the Vandals had moved into North Africa and ten years later they captured Carthage, which caused a further financial and supply crisis, that led to a failed attempt to re-cconquer the city in 468. The Huns finally crossed the frontier and attacked Constantinople, but couldn't breech its walls. On the guise of saving the Emperor's sister Honoria, Attila struck out to the Western Empire, only to be stopped at Chalons (Catalaunian Plains) in 451. In 476 Odoacer deposed the sixteen year old Romulus Augustulus and sent the

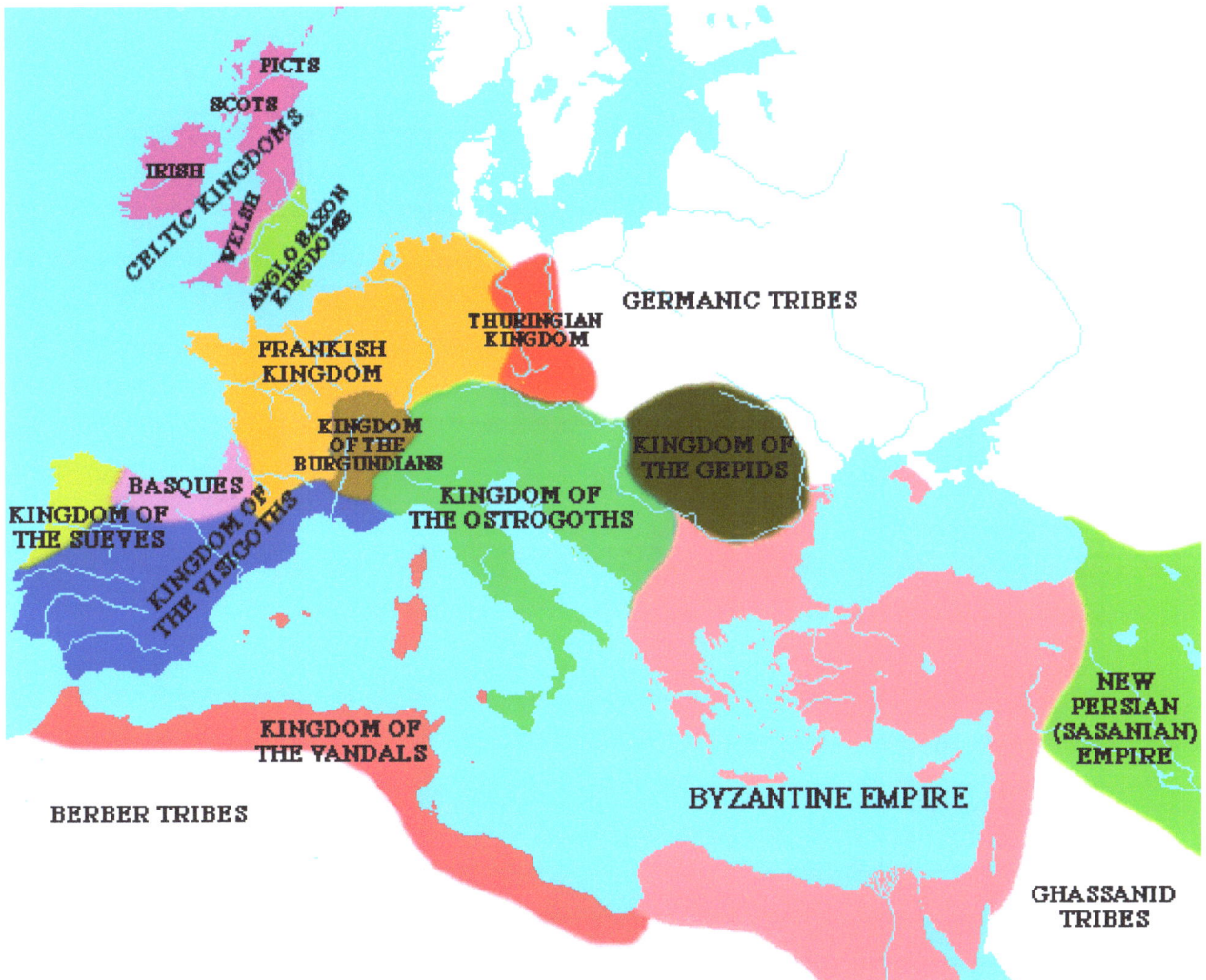

Fig 19. Europe in the 6th Century (Wikipedia)

Imperial insignia to Constantinople as a sign of submission to the eastern Emperor. This is traditionally acknowledged as the end of the Western Empire, but various usurpers continued to function under the claim of being "heirs" of the Empire. In 490, the Emperor Zeno granted Odoacer the position of Viceroy of Italia, which presupposed some sort of control. Following this, Theodoric the Great (King of the Ostrogoths) vied with Odoacer for favor from Constantinople and eventually killed him at a banquet to celebrate their joint rule. Theodoric in turn acted as an independent Viceroy in Italy for the eastern Emperor, until he eventually did away with any pretense of fidelity.

GABRIELE ESPOSITO

The Organization of the Late Roman Army

The evolution of the Roman military from the fourth to sixth centuries parallels the political, economic and social changes occurring in the Empire during the same period. Although the forces of the early Empire are often portrayed as the epitome of professionalism because of their constant employment, the army of the late period might be regarded as more professional than previously.

The Emperor Diocletian separated the military and civilian administrations, which were previously dual roles, creating a deep division between the civilian aristocratic elite and the military officer corps bringing each to focus on one aspect of what was a multifaceted position. The former had the advantage of wealth, lands and classical education, serving in the upper reaches of the civilian administration; the latter often rose from the lower ranks, as evidenced by the origins of many late Roman generals and Emperors. In fact, rank and file soldiers could become officers more easily than in earlier periods if they distinguished themselves in action.

The late Roman army was still a professional force of soldiers who were recruited, trained, supplied and paid by the state through a large and expensive bureaucracy, which still had preplanned budgets. The support of the military was in fact the single greatest expenditure of the Roman state. Despite this, the society of the late Empire was still a "non-militarized" one, in which there was a well-defined distinction between soldiers and civilians as opposed to a military society like that of the Spartans or the early Middle Ages. One possible reason behind this division was to keep those who pay the troops from those who led them.

The hierarchy of the late Empire for the Army and the Administration was set up as:

	Army	Administration
Praetorian Prefecture	Augustus/Caesar	Praefectus Praetorio
Diocese	Comes	Vicarius
Province	Dux	Corrector

In the 4th and early 5th centuries, ordinary citizens of the great metropolitan centers of the Empire (Rome, Alexandria and Constantinople) and most peasants of the interior provinces would have had little if any dealings with soldiers. The social status of the rank and file soldier was quite low during the late Empire and, despite theoretically good pay, Roman citizens preferred to avoid military service if they could. The revised social separation impacted the structure of the late Roman chain of command, which worked as follows: a small number of supreme generals, the magistri militum, were appointed to interact with the civil branch of government, in order to maximize the bureaucracy of organization and supply. They were second only to the Emperor and created some sort of military high command. Although they were legally appointed by the Emperors, they often held power over their nominal masters. In several instances, Emperors who felt threatened by their magistri militum organized their assassinations, which was easier than dismissing them. Comites (counts) and duces (dukes) were appointed to act as regional commanders, for the field and frontier forces respectively, while unit commanders were under their direct orders.

By the mid-third century Roman armies were no longer composed of men organized in traditional legions of the late Republic or early Principate: that kind of military organization had completely disappeared during the political and military chaos of the so-called "Third Century Crisis" (235-284 AD).

Fig 20. The Battle of the Milvian Bridge, fought on 28 October 312. The picture shows the terrible clash between the cataphracts of Maxentius and the legionaries of Constantine. Note the "draco" standard carried by the heavy cavalry and, in the background, the labarum (military vexillum) of Constantine: this displays the "Chi-Rho" sign and the words "IN HOC SIGNO VINCES", which were part of the famous "Vision of Constantine". (Giuseppe Rava)

Despite some superficial continuity, in the terminology which was used, the structure of the Roman army which emerged after the end of the crisis was totally different from the previous one.

The size of the army during this period has been the subject of conjecture in recent years. The most recent estimates have placed the army at between 250,000 to 300,000 from Constantine until the end of the Empire. The size of units also varied during this period, from era to era, as well as location.

Cavalry		Infantry	
Vexillatio	650	*Legio*	1,000
Ala	600	*Cohors*	500
Cuneus	250	*Numerous*	650
Schola	500		

Formations and Units

Limitanei and Comitatenses

The new organization of the Roman army started its development before the end of the "Third Century Crisis". In fact, during the year 268 AD (under the Emperor Gallienus), the first comitatensis field army was created combining detachments from legions and cavalry units. Although initially it was just a temporary force stationed in the province of Illyria, it would soon become permanent: the late Roman army was, in effect, born from this formation. The next major development in the structure of the Roman military can be credited to Constantine the Great, who formed the Gallic Field Army with the Gallic and British legions in 312. This comitatensis army numbered somewhere around 100,000 soldiers at that time, but was soon transferred to protect Italy. In order to keep the western provinces of the Empire well defended, Constantine took the legions and old auxilia units stationed on the Rhine frontier and created the riparienses, the first formal limitanei units.

By 324 AD, the Empire had several field armies and Constantine's changes had been applied across its whole territory. However, it is highly probable that Constantine only finished a program of military reforms created and started by Diocletian. Unfortunately the evidence for Diocletian's activities is scanty and the sources we have for his period are inconsistent: as a result, it is very difficult to say who was responsible for innovations, if Diocletian or Constantine. By 386, the classification of the border garrisons as limitanei was established in Roman records. By 395, the changes had become permanent and formal, which was one possible reason for the creation of the Notitia Dignitatum.

The Notitia Dignitatum as it exists today is believed to be a Roman administrative document listing all the units in the Eastern and Western Empire. The manuscripts we have today are fifteenth century copies of older documents, illustrated with the shield designs of western units up to 410 and eastern units up to 395.

By the late fourth century all the units of the Roman army were divided into two groups, which had different functions: the limitanei (frontier troops) and comitatenses (field forces). The former were stationed in a system of fortifications along the borders of the Empire, while the latter were mobile forces garrisoned in the regions deemed most vulnerable to attack. The limitanei were designed to react to and discourage low intensity threats, like raiding across the border. They were also used to impede the progress of major incursions, in order to allow sufficient time for the comitatenses to respond and intercept the invaders. Limitanei have often been portrayed as second class soldiers: this is partly true, because they had fewer privileges and tax breaks than the comitatenses. However, the limitanei were certainly not a poorly-equipped farmer militia, as is sometimes portrayed. They were additionally divided into three categories: burgarii, who maintained fortlets and watchtowers; castellani, who garrisoned forts; riparienses (or ripenses), who protected the Danube and Rhine frontier. A major difference between them appears to have revolved around the size of the unit, and to some extent equipment. In special circumstances, such as during an important military campaign, some units of the limitanei could be attached to the comitatensis army of their region, transforming them (albeit for a short period) into field units. When this happened, they were re-named as pseudocomitatenses.

As time went on, this temporary measure was increasingly used in a stable way and pseudocomitatenses units remained to serve with field armies for longer terms. By the year 450 AD, the limitanei were becoming increasingly tied to their garrisons, providing support against the invaders when the military operations happened to be within a short range, but unwilling to fight on fronts that were far from their homes. Unlike the field units, which increasingly had to recruit from barbarians, the limitanei remained mostly composed of Roman citizens. In the eastern Empire, the limitanei stationed on the Sassanid frontier would remain there until the war of 602 AD; the ones on the Danube, instead, were completely annihilated by Attila in 446 AD.

The comitatenses units were stationed in Gaul, Italy, Dalmatia, Moesia, Thrace, Asia Minor, Syria, Spain, Britain, Egypt and North Africa. Initially one of their most important functions was to counter barbarian incursions which the Empire increasingly faced during the last centuries of its existence. The comitatenses armies did not all exist at the same time and some were destroyed during the military campaigns of the late Empire. The British Field Army was absorbed into the Gallic Army in 405 AD, while we know that the Spanish one was destroyed before the last updating of the Notitia Dignitatum in 419. In 432 AD, the African Field Army was disbanded and used to replenish the Italic Field Army. Between 441 and 447, the Thracian and Illyrian Field Armies in the Balkans had all been destroyed by Attila's Huns. In addition to the regional Field Armies, the comitatenses units comprised also the so-called Comitatus Praesentalis, which was the Emperor's own central Field Army ("the army in the Imperial presence").

Around 365 AD, the distinction between this central army and the other comitatenses units had become clear. Initially it was under direct control of the Emperor, but later its command was given to a Magister Militum Praesentalis. The central Field Army was formed of higher quality and status units, which were generally known as palatini. In particular, it comprised the following kinds of units: legiones palatinae (heavy infantry), auxilia palatina (elite infantry) and vexillationes palatinae (cavalry).

During the mid-third century, Rome's defensive strategy experienced serious difficulties on all fronts. The Emperors Diocletian and Maximian tried to rebuild it by strengthening the elite field forces of their armies. On the Danubian limes and in the eastern Empire, Diocletian perfected the traditional system of picked legionary drafts, the legiones palatinae. In the west, Maximian and his Caesar Constantius raised a new class of troops, the Germanic auxilia palatina. These acted as a front-line infantry force and had developed from the irregular units of semi-barbarian troops (originally called numeri) of earlier centuries. Some of the senior and probably oldest of these had special names such as Cornuti or Brachiati; others were named after the tribes from which they were recruited (many of these in eastern Gaul, or among the German barbarians). These units all became auxilia palatina when a distinction was drawn between them and the other comitatenses units around 365 AD. There is no direct evidence for the strength of an auxilium, but we can suppose that it may have been 600 or 700 men. Apparently, the auxilia seem to have lost their "barbarian" origins quite early. A hundred years later, in the lists of the Notitia Dignitatum, the auxilia palatina still loom as the bulk of the Imperial field armies.

Fig 21. Infantryman of the Batavi iuniores, an auxilia palatina unit under command of the magister equitum praesentalis in Gaul. The Batavi, a Germanic tribe that lived around the modern Dutch Rhine delta, provided the Romans with contingents of warriors since the early days of the Empire: in fact, the majority of the Germani Corporis Custodes were from this tribe. The Notitia lists, in addition to the Batavi seniores and Batavi iuniores, other 5 units with the term "Batavi" in their title: Equites Batavi seniores, Equites Batavi iuniores, Laeti Batavi et gentiles Suevi, Laeti Batavi Nemetacenses, Laeti Batavi Contraginnenses. (Giuseppe Rava)

Foederati and Bucellarii

In addition to the split between field and frontier forces, there were also other two classes of troops: the foederati and the bucellarii. During the early centuries of the Empire, the majority of barbarian soldiers who were recruited into the Roman army were dispersed amongst various units, in order to be trained and fielded as professional Roman soldiers albeit having auxiliary duties. However, around 380 AD, this practice started to change as barbarian leaders began to retain a higher degree of independence and control over their warriors as semi-autonomous groups. As a result, by 450 AD, Aetius' Gallic army was heavily supported by independent contingents of Franks, Heruls, Huns, Goths, Burgundians and Alans. Although in some cases these troops continued to serve in Roman units, the majority of them were by now under command of their own tribal leaders, who were part of the administrative structure of the Roman lands where they were settled.

Gradually, the "allied" barbarian forces got more powerful, more independent and more dangerous. This was the basis of the famous "barbarization" of the Roman army: a complete replacement of Roman troops by barbarian foederati, who became the real masters of the Empire. The bucellarii, instead, were private armies of barbarian mercenaries at the orders of Roman commanders. The Latin term literally meant "biscuit-eaters", deriving from the name of their ration (the bucellatum, a type of dry

Fig 22. Dura-Europos synagogue soldiers in armor

34

biscuit). They were not supported by the central state, but were personally recruited by commanders, in essence being their personal troops. For example, Aetius is reported to have had large numbers of Huns and Goths serving him, thanks to his political connections. The same Galla Placidia had a corps of Gothic bodyguards, which were later converted into auxilia palatina unit, the Placidi Valentiniani. The units of bucellarii were generally quite small; however, during the many civil wars, they could grow to number several thousand men. Because they were equipped and paid for by wealthy and influential people, the bucellarii were quite often better trained and motivated than the regular soldiers. They held a personal loyalty to their officers and were much more reliable than the foederati for this reason. These soldiers had an important role during the last years of the Western Roman Empire, killing Emperors and supporting usurpers, but also playing a crucial part in several important battles.

Scholae Palatinae and Protectores

For centuries the Roman Emperors had been protected by the famous Praetorian Guard, but since the reign of Diocletian there were attempts by the Emperors to reduce its numbers and cancel some of its privileges. During the civil wars of the late Tetrarchy, the Emperor Severus II had already attempted to disband the Praetorian Guard, but only managed to lead them to revolt and joining Maxentius' forces. Later when Constantine defeated Maxentius at the Milvian Bridge in 312, the Praetorians made up a large portion of Maxentius' army. Subsequently Constantine was able to disband the Praetorian Guard (including the mounted branch of the Equites singulares Augusti) and break the cycle of privilege. Some time after this, guard units began to be referenced as the Scholae Palatinae. Although there is no direct evidence that Constantine established the Scholae Palatinae, the lack of a bodyguard unit would have become immediately apparent: this is the reason why he is commonly regarded as their founder. Some Scholae Palatinae units, like the Schola Gentilium, appear in records much earlier than 312 and may have their origins in the reign of Diocletian, but perhaps not as the same guard status as they later assumed.

The term schola was commonly used in the early 4th century to refer to organized corps of the imperial retinue, both civil and military, deriving from the fact that they occupied specific chambers in the imperial palace. Each Schola Palatina was an elite cavalry vexillatio of around 500 soldiers. The majority of these were recruited from among the Germanic tribes: in the western Empire, they were mainly composed of Franks and Alemanni. In the Eastern Empire Goths were the predominant tribe; however, from the mid-5th century, they were largely replaced with Armenians and Isaurians as a result of the anti-Gothic policies. In any case, the presence of native Romans in the scholae was also significant. Each schola was commanded by a tribunus, who ranked as a provincial dux. Unlike the Praetorian Guard, there was no overall military commander of the scholae: the Emperor retained direct control over them. For administrative purposes only, they were eventually placed under the direction of the magister officiorum. Originally there were a total of five scholae, but when the Empire was formally divided they were increased to ten (five for each half of the Empire). At the time of the *Notitia Dignitatum*, however, those of the eastern Empire had been augmented to seven. The following units of Scholae Palatinae are listed in the *Notitia Dignitatum*:

THE LATE ROMAN ARMY

Western Empire

    Schola scutariorum prima
    Schola scutariorum secunda
    Schola scutariorum tertia
    Schola armaturarum seniorum
    Schola gentilium seniorum

Eastern Empire

    Schola scutariorum prima
    Schola scutariorum secunda
    Schola scutariorum clibanariorum
    Schola scutariorum sagittariorum
    Schola armaturarum iuniorum
    Schola gentilium seniorum

Fig 23. Gothic cavalry. The impact of heavy cavalry charges was one of the key factors leading to Gothic victory at the Battle of Adrianople. The heavy cavalrymen of this picture are equipped with lorica hamata or lorica squamata, plus a wide range of different helmets. The light cavalrymen, instead, only have round shields for personal protection. (Giuseppe Rava)

As clear from their designations, there were three kinds of cavalrymen in the scholae units: Scutarii, Armaturae and Gentiles. The Scutarii were equipped as light cavalry but with large shields, hence their name. The Armaturae wore body armour and fought as heavy cavalry (similarly to the cataphractii). Regarding the Gentiles, we don't have any info about their equipment; however we know that they were all non-Roman soldiers, because the Latin word gentiles meant "foreigners" or "barbarians". So it is highly probable that they were guardsmen of Germanic origins.

The Schola scutariorum clibanariorum and the Schola scutariorum sagittariorum, which were the two extra units of the east, have unorthodox denominations. What we know for sure is that the first was a unit of clibanarii (eastern heavy cavalry) and the second a unit of mounted archers. The term scutariorum in their name probably reflects only the guard status of these units: it seems very improbable for clibanarii and horse archers to have large shields.

As befitted their guards status, the soldiers of the scholae received higher pay and enjoyed more privileges than the regular army: they received extra rations (the so-called annonae civicae), were exempt from the recruitment tax (with the privilegiis scholarum) and were often used by the Emperors for civilian missions inside the Empire. Gradually, however, the ease of palace life and lack of actual campaigning

Fig 24. The Arch of Galerius showing soldiers in lorica squamata

Fig 25. Praetorian Guardsman of the early Empire. During the late Republic, it was a habit of many Roman generals to choose from their ranks a private force of soldiers to act as guards of their tent or person; in time, this elite cohort came to be known as the cohors praetoria. Various important generals possessed one, including Julius Caesar, Mark Antony and Octavian. When Augustus became the first ruler of the Roman Empire in 31 BC, he decided that such a formation would have been useful not only on the battlefield but in politics also. Thus, from the ranks of legions throughout the provinces, Augustus recruited the Praetorian Guard. Note the use of a muscle cuirass with pteruges, typical of Roman "guard" units. (Giuseppe Rava)

lessened their combat abilities, transforming them into parade-ground formations. This was also due to the fact that it became possible to buy an appointment into the ranks of the scholae: because of the social status and benefits that this entailed, they were increasingly filled with by Constantinople's well-connected young nobility. In the western Empire, they were permanently disbanded by Theodoric the Great in the 490's. In the eastern Empire, they were eventually replaced as the main imperial bodyguard by the Excubitores, created by the Emperor Leo I in 468 AD. These numbered 300 men, often recruited from among the Isaurians, as part of Leo's effort to counterbalance the influence of the large Germanic element in the eastern Roman army.

The Excubitores were billeted in the imperial palace itself and, for a certain period, formed the only garrison of Constantinople. Their high status is further illustrated by the fact that some of them were often sent for special missions by the Emperors, including diplomatic assignments. The unit was headed by the comes excubitorum, who, by virtue of his proximity to the Emperor, gradually became an official of great importance. An inner guard of just 40 men, picked from the Scholae Palatinae for their loyalty rather than as potential leaders, bore the brunt of the bodyguard function: these were the Candidati, whose name derived from the bright white tunics that they used to wear. They were commanded by a primicerius. Although by the 6th century they too fulfilled a purely ceremonial role, in the 4th century they accompanied the Emperors on campaign. In addition to the Scholae Palatinae, another kind of guard unit took the place of the Praetorians: the Protectores.

Originally, the title of Protector was given to individual officers of the Roman army as a mark of their devotion to and approval by the Emperor himself. It seems that, when it was first bestowed during the reign of Gallienus, this title signified an honour conferred on rather than a function carried out by the recipient. It was granted to officers (mainly tribuni or centuriones) who had distinguished themselves serving directly under the Emperor. These were men noticed by the Emperor and likely to receive accelerated promotion in his service. Collectively, therefore, the first Protectores were a guild or an order attached to the Imperial staff rather than a defined military unit serving a military purpose. There is reference to a princeps protectorum, but it is very probable that this officer's functions were only ceremonial.

After the death of Gallienus, the Protectores seem to have evolved into a proper military unit. This was divided into two corps: the Protectores and the Protectores domestici (also known as Domestici). The first were infantry soldiers, while the latter fought as elite cavalrymen. The majority of them were of Germanic origins. Both units were commanded by a comes domesticorum: the infantry by the comes domesticorum peditum, the cavalry by the comes domesticorum equitum. Similarly to the later Excubitores, they were often used for special missions by the Emperor: in that case they were known as deputati. In practice, they served both as bodyguards and staff officers to the Emperor. After a few years' service in the corps, a domesticus would normally be granted a commission by the Emperor and placed in command of a military unit.

In addition to the above there was also a unit known as the Germani Corporis Custodes. This elite corps of Germanic bodyguards was formed by the Emperor Augustus and continued to serve under the subsequent Emperors of the Julio-Claudian dynasty (30 BC – 60 AD). In contrast to the Praetorians, the Germani were a unit of personal guards recruited from distant parts of the Empire, with no political or personal connections with Rome. For this reason they were valued as loyal and reliable by the Emperors, who used them to counter the ambitions of the Praetorian Guard. They proved remarkably devoted to the Emperors, even to Caligula, whose death they avenged by beheading as many conspirators as they could find. The 500 bodyguards of this unit were formed up in five centuries, each being commanded by a Roman centurion. The Germani were disbanded for a brief period after the disaster of the Teutoburg Forest, reformed and finally dissolved by Galba in 68 AD, because of their loyalty to Nero (whom Galba

Fig. 26 Candidatus, one of the 40 elite guardsmen chosen from the Scholae Palatinae to form the personal bodyguard of the Emperor. Note the bright white tunic typical of this unit: it has very rich decorations, including complex clavii and orbiculi. The manufacture of the cloak and boots is excellent. (Giuseppe Rava)

had overthrown). A unit under that name was reformed in the early 3rd century and continued to protect Emperors until the fall of the Empire in the west. Germanic mercenaries were very popular as bodyguards during the 5th century: even the Pope had a certain number of Germanic guards protecting his person, who were the first soldiers serving in the army of the Papal States.

Laeti

Laeti was a term used in the late Roman Empire to denote communities of barbarians who were permitted to settle on Imperial territory, on condition that they provided recruits for the Roman military. The term laetus is of uncertain origin: it means "happy" in Latin, but may derive from a Germanic word meaning "half-free colonist". Laeti may have been groups of migrants drawn from the tribes that lived beyond the Empire's borders. These had been in constant contact and intermittent warfare with the Empire since its northern borders were stabilized during the reign of Augustus in the early 1st century. In the west, these tribes were primarily Germans, living beyond the Rhine.

Although the literary sources only mention laeti from the 4th century onwards, it is likely that their forebearers existed from as early as the 2nd century. The 3rd-century historian Dio Cassius reports

Fig 27. Dura Europos fresco of Roman troops (Wikipedia)

Fig 28. Protector, equipped as a heavy infantryman. This elite soldier carries all the best pieces of equipment available: Spangenhelm, lorica squamata with pteruges, spatha and round shield with the "Chi-Rho" emblem. (Giuseppe Rava)

that Emperor Marcus Aurelius granted land on the border regions to groups of Marcomanni, Quadi and Iazyges who had been captured during the Marcomannic Wars and resettled in Germania, Pannonia, Moesia, Dacia and Italy. Marcus Aurelius later expelled those who settled on the Italian peninsula after one group mutinied and briefly seized Ravenna, the base of the Adriatic fleet. These early settlers may have been the original laeti. There is evidence that the practice of settling communities of barbarians inside the Empire stretches as far back as the Emperor Augustus himself. During his time, a number of subgroups of Germanic tribes from the eastern bank of the Rhine were transferred, at their own request, to the Roman-controlled western bank. In 69 AD, the Emperor Otho is reported to have settled communities of Mauri from North Africa in the province of Hispania Baetica. Given the existance of several auxiliary regiments with the names of these tribes in the 1st and 2nd centuries, it is likely that their admission to the Empire was conditional on some kind of military obligations.

The precise constitution which regulated laeti settlements is still not clear. It is possible that their organization was standard, or alternatively that the terms varied with each individual settlement. There is also doubt about whether the terms governing laeti were distinct from those applying to gentiles ("natives"), dediticii ("surrendered barbarians") or tributarii (peoples obliged to pay tribute). It is possible that these names were used interchangeably, or at least overlapped considerably. On the other hand, they may refer to juridically distinct types of community, with distinct sets of obligations and privileges for each type. Most likely, the terms laeti and gentiles were interchangeable, as they are listed in the same section of the "Notitia Dignitatum", both referring to voluntary settlements. In addition, the Notitia often places the two terms together.

Fig 29. Decurion of the Germani Corporis Custodes, reign of Nero. An important characteristic of this corps was its private and unofficial character. In fact, in organization and status, it was part of the monarch's household rather than a component of the Empire's military establishment. This was in line with the distinction maintained during the Principate between servants of the Emperor and officials of the state. (Giuseppe Rava)

Prosperous groups of laeti (including women and children) would be granted land (terrae laeticae) to settle in the Empire by the Imperial government. They appear to have formed distinct military cantons, which probably were outside the normal provincial administration, since the settlements were under the control of a Roman praefectus laetorum (or praefectus gentilium), who was probably a military officer, as he reported to the magister peditum praesentalis in Italy. In the late 4th/early 5th centuries this officer was effectively the supreme commander of the western Roman Army. In return for their privileges of admission to the Empire and land grants, the laeti settlers were under an obligation to supply recruits to the Roman Army, with a greater proportions of conscripts liable for service than ordinary communities of the late Empire. The treaty granting a laeti community land might specify a once-and-for-all contribution of recruits, or a fixed number of recruits required each year.

There has been some recent discussion about whether recruits from laeti settlements formed their own distinct military units or were simply part of the general pool of army recruits. The traditional view of scholars is that the praefecti laetorum or gentilium mentioned in the Notitia were each in command of a regiment composed of the laeti. Some scholars argue that laeti were normally drafted into existing military units and only rarely formed their own. The main support for this view is a decree of 400 AD contained in the "Codex Theodosianus", which authorises a magister militum praesentalis to enlist Alemanni and Sarmatian laeti, together with other groups such as the sons of veterans. This probably implies that laeti were seen as part of the general pool of recruits. In this case, the praefecti laetorum/gentilium may have been purely administrative roles, especially charged with ensuring the full military levy from their cantons each year.

Much of our information on laeti contained in the "Notitia Dignitatum" mentions laeti settlements in Italy and Gaul, but it suggests that laeti settlements may have existed in the Danubian provinces also. The Notitia contains two lists of laeti prefects, one for the praefecti laetorum in Gaul and one for the praefecti gentilium Sarmatarum (prefects of Sarmatian gentiles) in Italy and Gaul. The Notitia contains thirty-fout entries concerning laeti, but some entries relate to several settlements and not just one (for example, the Sarmatian settlements in Apulia and Calabria). Furthermore, more than two pages of entries relating to laeti appear to be missing from the text. The number of settlements may thus have been in the hundreds, in the western half of the Empire only.

Praefecti laetorum in Gaul:

      Batavi and Suevi at Baiocas (Bayeux, Normandy) and Constantia (Coutances, Normandy)
      Suevi at Ceromannos (Le Mans, Maine) and Arumbernos (Auvergne)
      Franci at Redonas (Rennes, Brittany)
      Teutoniciani at Carnunta (Chartres, Maine)
      Lingones dispersed over Belgica I province
      Acti at Epuso, in Belgica I
      Nervii at Fanomantis (Famars, Picardy)
      Batavi Nemetacenses at Atrabatis (Arras, Picardy)
      Batavi Contraginnenses at Noviomagus (Nijmegen, Netherlands)
      Lagenses near Tungri (Tongres, Belgium)
      Unspecified gentiles at Remo (Reims, Champagne) and Silvamectum (Senlis)

Praefecti gentilium Sarmatarum in Italy:
- Apulia and Calabria
- Lucania and Bruttii
- Forum Fulviense
- Opittergum (modern Oderzo)
- Patavium (modern Padua)
- Cremona
- Taurini (modern Turin)
- Aquae sive Tertona (modern Tortona)
- Novaria (modern Novara)
- Vercellae (modern Vercelli)
- Regio Samnites (modern Sannio, a region of southern Italy)
- Bononia (modern Bologna)
- Quadratae and Eporizium (in modern Friuli, a region of northern Italy)
- Pollentia (modern Pollenzo)

Praefecti gentilium Sarmatarum in Gaul:
- Pictavi (modern Poitiers)
- Chora Parisios (Paris region)
- Remos and Ambianos in Belgica II (Champagne region)
- Tractum Rodunensem et Alaunorum (Rennes region)
- Lingones (modern Langres)

The Notitia also mentions a tribunus gentis Marcomannorum under the command of the dux Pannoniae et Norici and a tribunus gentis per Raetias deputatae ("tribune of natives in the Raetian provinces"). These Marcomanni were probably laeti and may be the descendants of the peoples settled in the area by Marcus Aurelius during the 2nd century. Additionally, they may have been descended from Germans settled in Pannonia following Gallienus' treaty with King Attalus of the Marcomanni in AD 258.

Types of Military Units

Unfortunately, the military terminology used in late Roman sources is less precise than in earlier periods. The basic units for infantry were the legio, the numerus and the cohortis; those for cavalry were the vexillatio, the ala and the cuneus. Determining size and organization of these new units has been a matter of debate for some time, but the most modern theory regarding this subject, going through the individual unit sizes and their subsequent organization, is as follows:

The Legio was the name carried over from the old Roman legion, but at this time it was far smaller and more versatile: according to the works of Claudian and Orosius, it seemed to number about 1,000 soldiers (960 men plus the staff officers). Each legion was usually organized on 12 centuries, possibly divided into two cohorts. It was almost always commanded by a praefectus legionis, but sometimes a legion of the limitanei could be commanded by a praepositus. Underneath the praefectus there were the primicerius (or Lieutenant Commander) and several vicarii as well, who were temporary or staff officers. These could replace the praefectus or primicerius if they were killed in battle or not present to command.

Fig 30. The Herculiani iuniores, one of the legiones palatinae under command of the magister militum praesentalis I in the eastern Empire. This picture gives a very good idea of how a late Roman legion looked like. On the right you can see an officer wearing a leather muscle cuirass, with plumbatae being carried on the back of his shield. Note, in the background, a "draco" standard and the archers with pileus pannonicus. (Giuseppe Rava)

Underneath the primicerius was the domesticus (or Chief of Staff) and underneath him were the campidoctor and senator (respectively Drillmaster and Herald). The former seems to have taken a similar role to the old primus pilus or praefectus castrorum. Next came the centurions, by now commonly known as centenarii; underneath the centurion there was the biarchus, who commanded half a century. The single century was organized into ten contubernia, each one being commanded by a decanus. The subordinate ranks of the late legions were quite similar to those of the earlier Empire: in contemporary sources we still find optiones (centurion's deputies) and tesserarii (watch officers). New ranks, attested from the later 3rd century, would include actuarius (legion quartermaster), adiutor (record keeper) and draconarius (the bearer of the "windsock" draco standard). It appears that some units still kept an eagle, but the draco often replaced these in the field – a device made more prevalent from the time of the Dacian wars.

By the mid-5th century, the majority of cohort-sized units had been replaced by new ones known as numeri. Each numerus numbered about 640 men plus staff officers, organized into 8 centuries. It was commanded by a tribunus, who had a primicerius and several vicarii under his command. Like the legio, each numerus also had a domesticus, a campidoctor and a senator. However, its internal structure was different: it was subdivided into 4 manipules, each commanded by a ducenarius with two centenarii at his orders. The rank of ducenarius, which began as an honorific title for centurions promoted into the Protectores, was later adopted to denote a senior unit commander.

The cohortis numbered about 480 men plus staff officers, organized into 6 centuries. It was commanded by a tribunus, with a primicerius, several vicarii, a domesticus, a campidoctor and a senator underneath him. Each century was commanded by an ordinarius, who was like a centurion but did not have the same privileges. Underneath the ordinarius there were the biarchus and ten decani. Milites was the general term indicating infantrymen, but was also used as a synonym of numeri.

In the late Republic and early Principate Cavalry was supplied by foreign auxilia as separate units. In the late Empire cavalry was fully integrated into the Roman military machine. Its tactical importance and battlefield prestige grew during the last centuries of the Empire, in part because of the encounters with nomadic horsed peoples such as the Huns, Persians and Sarmatians. The increased role of cavalry was the answer to the need for greater strategic and tactical mobility in the face of mobile enemies and decreased ability to defend in depth. In the early Empire, a vexillatio was a detachment from a legion: in fact, some legions had several detachments across the Empire, sometimes totalling up to 2,400 men. These could be both comitatenses or limitanei units. Over time the term vexillatio was increasingly used to indicate a large cavalry unit. In theory it should have had the same structure of the infantry numerus, but in practice there was much more flexibility. We have examples of vexillationes numbering thousands of cavalrymen and others having just 20 men.

According to Zozimus, the ala of the late Roman cavalry numbered 600 men; we are not completely sure about this figure, because other ancient authors like Ammianus and Julian mention alae of 350 men. The ala of the 4th century was ideally commanded by a tribunus and divided into 20 turmae of 30 men, each led by a decurio; which was pretty much the same since the days of the Principate. Eventually this was phased out during the end of the 5th century by the newer cunei.

Equites was the general term indicating cavalrymen, but was also used to indicate the size of a unit, created usually from old cavalry vexillationes. Ammianus mentions two units of equites being combined together in order to form an ala of 700 men, so it is also possible that each ala was divided into two equites. Either way, it is known that each equites unit was commanded by a tribunus.

The cuneus was the newest and most innovative unit of the late Roman army: in fact, it seems to have been influenced by the Hunnic military tradition. The Huns, famous for their cavalry composed of mounted archers, used a term similar to the latin word cuneus to describe their clan-based military organization. However, according to Arrian, it seems to have been a development of the tarantiarchia, which was a 256-man "half-ala". Therefore, it is possible that each cuneus was commanded by a tribunus and divided into eight 32-man turmae. Like in the vexillatio, each turma was commanded by a decurio. These cavalry units would additionally be designated as cataphractii, clibanarii and sagittarii.

Fig 31. Late Roman Officer and two soldiers ("The Great Hunt Mosaic", Villa Romana del Casale)

The Equites

Between 260 and 290 AD several new categories of cavalry unit were created, as part of the re-organization and expansion of the Roman cavalry forces initiated during the reign of Emperor Gallienus (260-268). The most innovative one was that of the equites stablesiani. The "*Notitia Dignitatum*" lists various units of equites stablesiani stationed throughout the Roman Empire, but units of this kind are also recorded at an earlier date, including an inscription on the "Deurne helmet". The origin of the equites stablesiani and the meaning of their name remain obscure. Some scholars suggest that these units were raised from a corps of grooms, originally attached to the new cavalry vexillationes created under Gallienus. It is probable that they were formed from soldiers who had previously been seconded to the staff of provincial governors as grooms and/or bodyguards. The equites stablesiani appear to have formed part of the Imperial field army during the military crisis of the 260s and 270s. Later, probably during the Tetrarchy period or the reign of Constantine I, most units of this class were permanently assigned to the garrisons of frontier provinces. The continued existence of some equites stablesiani units is attested well into the sixth century.

Another new category added to was that of the equites promoti: the term promoti means "advanced" or "promoted" and seems to have originally been applied to individual soldiers. As time went on, groups of such select legionaries appear to have been given training as horsemen (presumably as a sort of mounted infantry). This seemingly gave rise, especially during the 3rd century, to the formation of legionary cavalry units, which then seem to have been detached for use as independent units. The Notitia lists a large number of equites promoti units, albeit mostly in limitanei roles rather than serving with field armies. In fact, many of them are qualified as indigenae (which means "native"). The limitanei included also many cavalry units defined as equites sagittarii indigenae, which meant "native horse archers".

A third interesting group of units was that of the equites Dalmatae: these were the largest category of the new cavalry vexillationes. The earliest documentation regarding them relates to the reign of Gallienus. The titular component Dalmatae probably refers to the geographical region in which these units were raised and/or originally stationed, namely the provinces of the western Balkans which formed the core of Gallienus' truncated Empire. They possibly originated as detachments of alae and cohortes equitatae available to Gallienus in these provinces. The equites Dalmatae appear to have contributed to the victories of Aurelian during the reconquest of Palmyra. Subsequently, probably during the Tetrarchy period or the reign of Constantine I, most of the equites Dalmatae were permanently assigned to the garrisons of frontier provinces.

Late Roman Uniforms

Military Dress

The equipment of the late Roman Army was still supplied by the state as it was in previous centuries, and still standardized in consistent patterns. State factories produced military clothing, weapons and armour and the Imperial authorities provided rations and medical services to the soldiers. Cavalry mounts were raised in state farms. Our main source, the "Notitia Dignitatum", lists a total of 35 state "fabricae" located across the Empire at the beginning of the fifth century. As a result of this organization, we can state with some degree of certainty that the late Roman soldier was still uniformly equipped, as previous armies. As the economic and social decline of the Empire began to spiral downward, the quality and quantity of the provisions given to soldiers decreased.

By the end of the 4th century, for example, uniform issues were starting to be replaced by a clothing allowance. Generally speaking, the clothing of the comitatenses had a higher degree of uniformity than that of the limitanei: the latter probably bought their clothing from small local stores attached to their frontier forts, although there might have encompassed standard patterns then in use. As with the case of the "auxilia" of the previous centuries, the weapons and equipment of the limitanei were strongly influenced by those of the peoples living along the Roman frontiers (both inside and outside the Empire). Even if their stores were supplied (at least partly) by the state, the frontier troops most likely took on a certain amount of local flavour in their general appearance.

The clothing used by the soldiers of the field armies was surely of better quality and much more "standardized"; in any case, because comitatenses had no fixed bases and were almost always on campaign, regular supply from a fixed source would have been something practically impossible for them and they would begin to "go native" in local dress. The clothing allowance, in fact, was probably the result of an attempt to ease the logistical difficulties of re-supplying the field armies. After a long campaign the comitatenses units usually presented a very motley appearance, because they would have had to make local purchases quite regularly in order to replace their original pieces of equipment (the clothing supplied by the state did not last long in the field). In addition, especially during the 5th century, the clothing of the Roman soldiers was increasingly influenced by the military fashions of the foederati, who fought with them during the long campaigns of the late Empire.

Many different nationalities served side by side, influencing each other and introducing new items of dress in the Roman military clothing. Climate was another very important factor: the veterans of Julian's Gallic Army, having arrived in Antioch for the Persian campaign of 363 AD, were initially dressed with heavy north European clothing; this was clearly inadequate for the hot southern climate of Anatolia and Mesopotamia. Once the campaign begun, hot heavy items were soon discarded, to be replaced by local Persian clothing and pieces of equipment. The army that returned to Antioch after the campaign was thus very different from the one which had started the expedition some months before. Local peculiarities were very apparent in the dress and equipment of the limitanei, which was very diverse across the Empire. The appearance of a Gallic auxiliary had very little in common with that of an Arabian one serving on the desert frontier.

Roman military fashions underwent very gradual change from the late Republic to the end of the western Empire, in a process lasting for more than 500 years. After Diocletian's reforms, the clothing worn by soldiers and non-military government bureaucrats became highly decorated, with woven or embellished strips (clavi) and circular roundels (orbiculi) being added to tunics and cloaks. These decorative elements usually comprised geometrical patterns and stylised plant motifs, but could include human or animal figures. The use of silk increased steadily, with the result that most high officers wore elaborate silk robes. Heavy military-style belts were worn by soldiers as well as by bureaucrats, revealing some militarization in the clothing of the late Roman civilian government. Trousers, which were considered barbarous garments worn by Germans and Persians, achieved only limited popularity in the later days of the Empire, being regarded by conservatives as a sign of cultural decay.

Fig 32. From left to right: officer of the Armigeri defensores seniores, infantryman of the Tervingi, archer of the I Isaura sagittaria and cataphract. The officer wears a leather muscle cuirass with pteruges. The Armigeri defensores seniores were one of the legiones comitatenses under command of the magister equitum praesentalis in Gaul. The Tervingi, instead, were one of the auxilia palatina units under command of the magister militum praesentalis II in the eastern Empire. The archer, armed with wooden longbow, axe and small round shield, is from the I Isaura sagittaria: this was one of the pseudocomitatenses units at the orders of the magister militum per Orientem. It was clearly the first in a series of three units, since the Comes Isauriae included Legio II Isaura and Legio III Isaura; it is probable that the first Isaurian legion was withdrawn from the home province to be absorbed into the Comes Orientem. Legio I Isaura sagittaria is the only legion to be given the title of "sagittaria" in the Notitia Dignitatum, presumably because bow was the main weapon of the Isaurians (who lived in southern Anatolia). (Giuseppe Rava)

Military Equipment

Helmets

In the late 3rd century, the Roman helmet design deviated from age old patterns: previous helmet types, based mainly on Celtic designs, were replaced by new forms deriving from helmets developed in the Sassanid Empire. These new models are known under the generic term of "ridge helmets", because they were characterized by the possession of a bowl made up of two or four parts, united by a longitudinal ridge. A Sassanid helmet from the 3rd century, found in Dura Europos, seems to be the model that later Roman "ridge helmets" were based on. The earliest confirmed example of a late Roman ridge helmet is the "Richborough helmet", which dates to about 280 AD. During those years, the Romans adopted two main forms of helmet construction: one was the ridge helmet, the other was the so-called "Spangenhelm" (which was likely adopted from the Sarmatians).

The skull of the ridge helmet differed from earlier "Gallic" helmets in that it was constructed from more than one element. Roman ridge helmets can be classified into two types of skull construction: bipartite and quadripartite, also referred to as "Intercisa-type" and "Berkasovo-type", respectively. The bipartite construction method was usually characterized by a two-part bowl united by a central ridge, running from front to back, and by small cheekpieces. It lacked a base-ring running around the rim of the bowl. Some examples of the bipartite construction also utilized metal crests, such as in the "Intercisa-IV" and "River Maas" helmets. The quadripartite construction method was characterized by a four-piece bowl connected by a central ridge, with two plates (connected by a reinforcing band) on each side of the ridge and a base-ring uniting the elements of the skull at the rim of the helmet. This type of helmet is characterised by large cheekpieces. Many helmets of this kind also have a nasal. It is generally believed that the cheekpieces were attached to skull by a helmet liner and that the separate neck guard was attached by flexible leather straps, as indicated by the buckles which survive on some helmets. There are, however, notable exceptions to this classification method: these include the "Iatrus" and "Worms" helmets, which have large cheekpieces and a base ring respectively.

Earlier Roman cavalry helmet types usually had cheek guards with a section covering the ears, whereas infantry helmets did not. Some historians have extrapolated from this that the "Intercisa-type" helmets were infantry ones, while the "Berkasovo-type" were cavalry helmets, using as evidence the existence of ear-holes in the "Intercisa-type". In addition, one "Berkasovo-type" helmet (the so-called "Deurne helmet") has an inscription related to a cavalry unit of the Equites Stablesiani, lending to support this theory. Both types of

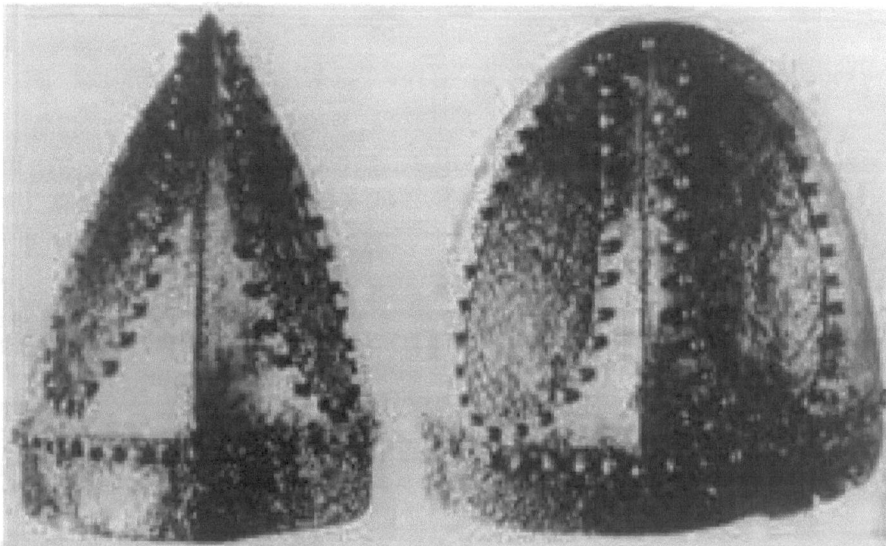

Fig 33. Early form of Sassanid Spangenhelm from Dura Europos

ridge helmets, however, are depicted on infantry and cavalry in late Roman art. Some evidence, such as the "Burgh Castle" helmet, shows that they were used interchangeably. Late Roman ridge helmets are first depicted on coins of Constantine the Great and are believed to have come into use between 270 and 300 AD. The last archaeological examples date to the early 5th century, including the "River Maas Helmet", dated to 409-411 by coins of Constantine III. Early copies of ridge helmets include the "Fernpass" example, dated to the 4th century and found in Austria, which is believed to belong to a Germanic warrior who had his own helmet modified to look like a ridge helmet. Many helmets of the new Germanic Kingdoms of western and northern Europe in the early Middle Ages were derivations of the Roman ridge helmet, for example the Anglo-Saxon "Coppergate Helmet".

The Spangenhelm arrived in Western Europe by way of what is now southern Russia and Ukraine,

Fig 34. Roman Spangenhelm from Deir el-Medina

Fig. 35. Early ridge helmet

being spread by nomadic tribes like the Scythians and the Sarmatians. While Roman contact with these peoples originates in the 1st century, as these troops were incorporated into Roman cavalry units, their fashions influenced later development. The word, "Spangenhelm", instead, is of Germanic origin: spangen refers to the metal strips that form the framework of the helmet and could be translated as "braces", while helm simply means "helmet". The strips connect three to six steel or bronze plates and the frame takes a conical design that curves with the shape of the head, culminating in a point. The front of the helmet may include a nasal. Spangenhelms could also incorporate mail as neck protection, thus forming a partial aventail. Some include eye protection in a shape that resembles modern eyeglass frames; others include a full face mask. Older Spangenhelms often had cheek flaps made from metal or leather. In general, the Spangenhelm was an effective protection for the head that was relatively easy to produce. Weakness of the design was its partial head protection and its jointed construction. By the 6th century it was the most common helmet design in Europe and in popular use throughout the Middle East. They were used for a very long period, being later replaced by similarly shaped helmets, made with one-piece skulls: the famous "Nasal Helmets". Some of these, depicted on the Bayeux Tapestry from the 11th century, appear to be built as a Spangenhelm construction.

Based on surviving examples there is evidence that some helmets included decorative silvering or were covered by costly silver or silver-gilt sheathing. The job of decorating helmets was entrusted to special artisans known as barbaricarii. In some cases, like the "Berkasovo-I", the helmet was decorated with many glass gems on the bowl, cheekpieces and neckguard.

Fig 36. Modern reconstruction of an eastern auxiliary archer helmet from the early Empire (Armor venue)

Fig 37. Modern reconstruction of a late Roman ridge helmet

Fig 38. Late Roman ridge helmet (Berkasovo-type), early 4th century AD. Made of iron and sheathed in silver-gilt; decorated with glass gems. From the "Berkasovo treasure" and now in Novi Sad (Serbia)

Fig 39. Modern replica of a ridge helmet of the Intercisa IV type, presumably used by infantry officers

Fig 40. Modern reconstruction of an infantry ridge helmet

Fig 41. Late Roman ridge helmet (Berkasovo-type) from Deurne, Netherlands. It is covered in silver-gilt sheaeing and bears an inscription related to the Equites Stablesiani

Armor

The question of how much armor was worn by the late Roman Army has been a matter of discussion amongst historians since many years. According to the "De Re Militari" of Vegetius:

"...For though after the example of the Goths, the Alans and the Huns, we have made some improvements in the arms of the cavalry, it is plain that the infantry are entirely defenceless. From the foundation of the city until the reign of the Emperor Gratian, the foot wore cuirasses and helmets. But negligence and slothfulness having by degrees introduced a total relaxation of discipline, the soldiers began to consider their armour too heavy and seldom put it on. They first requested leave from the Emperor to lay aside the cuirass and afterwards the helmet. In consequence of this, our troops in their engagements with the Goths were often overwhelmed with their showers of arrows..."

Vegetius attributes this "negligence and slothfulness" to the soldiers and later on to the Imperial military system in general. The general tone of Vegetius is "we don't do things as well today as we used to..." For a long time, the claims of this author have been generally accepted as fact. Now, thanks to recent research, we have a greater understanding of the period and can settle the debate in more precise terms. Both before and after Vegetius, we have strong evidence that the Roman heavy infantrymen wore metal body armor and helmet. Ammianus Marcellinus, who was himself a soldier, makes frequent reference in his works to 4th century infantry wearing armour, describing the legionaries at Adrianople as *weighed down by the burden of their armor*. Luckily we have many examples of material evidence to support this view, dating back from the beginning of the late Roman period up to the fall of the western Empire. The 3rd century Arch of Galerius shows infantrymen in armor, as well as some Egyptian carvings from the 5th and 6th centuries. The arch of Galerius shows armor as scale, chainmail and leather cuirasses.

Fig 42. Gothic style armor

Fig 43. Late Roman lorica hamata on a re-enactor (wikipedia)

However, Vegetius' claims can be partially explained bearing in mind the material losses suffered by the Empire during the later parts of the 4th century against the Persians and Goths. Other factors supporting Vegetius' view could be the increasing use of foederati in the late Roman armies (who usually had no armor) and the already mentioned introduction of allowances in place of issued equipment, which may have resulted in no armor. In any case, for most of his service the late Roman soldier would have no need to wear armour. Marches were usually conducted with armour carried in wagons; guard duty, scouting, foraging expeditions and skirmishing were all conducted without wearing armour. The complete equipment was worn only to fight in line of battle. To sum up, it seems reasonable to assume that the late Roman infantryman wore metal body armor and a helmet when fighting in line of battle, whether he was part of a legion or of an auxilia palatina unit. When on patrol, on guard duty, on the march or fighting as a skirmisher he left most of his armour off, acting as light infantry. The changing role of infantry within the tactical thinking of the later western Empire may have moved the infantry to lighten their load – trading defense for maneuverability. In the east, however, the way infantry was used may have necessitated keeping heavier armored troops. At the time of Justinian many infantry units were still wearing full armour.

Fig 44. Late Roman lorica squamata

Fig 45. Lorica squamata

The armor worn by the late Roman soldiers could be of three main different types: the lorica hamata, the lorica squamata (scale) or the muscle cuirass. The traditional lorica segmentata, which was worn by the famous legionaries sculpted on Trajan's Column, disappeared from Roman use during the 3rd century, most likely due to its high cost and difficult maintenance. It appears to have still been in use into the early 4th century, being depicted in the Arch of Constantine erected in 315; however, it has been argued that these depictions are from an earlier monument by Marcus Aurelius, from which Constantine incorporated portions into his Arch.

Since the beginning of the Empire, the auxilia had always been equipped with the lorica hamata instead of the lorica segmentata. The former was a type of mail armor mostly manufactured out of bronze or iron. It comprised alternating rows of closed washer-like rings punched from iron sheets and rows of riveted rings made from drawn wire that ran horizontally, producing very flexible, reliable and strong armour. Each ring had an inside diameter of about 5 mm and an outside diameter of about 7 mm. Up to 30,000 rings would have gone into one lorica hamata and the estimated production time was two months, even with continual slave labor at the state-run armouries. Although labor-intensive to manufacture, it is thought that, with good maintenance, this kind of armor could be used for several decades. Constant friction kept the rings of the lorica hamata free of rust, unlike the lorica segmentata which needed constant maintenance to prevent corrosion. By the 4th century AD it was the standard-issue armour of the Roman Army. These later versions of the lorica hamata had sleeves and covered the legs to the knees.

The lorica squamata was a type of scale armour made from small metal scales sewn to a fabric backing. The individual scales (squamae) were either iron or bronze, or even alternating metals on the same shirt. They could be tinned as well, one surviving fragment showing bronze scales that were alternately tinned and plain. The metal was generally not very thick, 0.50 mm to 0.80 mm being a common range. Since the scales overlapped in every direction, however, the multiple layers gave good protection. Scales could have rounded, pointed or flat bottoms with the corners clipped off at an angle. They could be flat, or slightly domed, or have a raised midrib/edge. The scales were wired or laced together in horizontal rows that were then laced or sewn to the backing. Therefore, each scale had from four to 12 holes: two or more at each side for wiring to the next in the row, one or two at the top for fastening to the backing and sometimes one or two at the bottom to secure the scales to the backing or to each other. The lorica squamata was particularly popular in the eastern half of the Empire, due to the military influence of the Empire's eastern enemies.

The muscle cuirass was a type of body armour cast to fit the wearer's torso and designed to mimic an idealized human body. These cuirasses were cast in two pieces, the front and the back, and then hammered. During the late Empire, simpler versions were preferred, with the anatomy being reduced to an abstract design. The cuirasses of Emperors and high ranking officers were often highly ornamented with mythological scenes or other kinds of rich decorations. Usually it was used in combination with fringed leather (pteruges) at the armholes and lower edge. The muscle cuirass was worn mostly by officers, being a sign of their rank. The Columns of Arcadius and Theodosius, as well as other examples from late Roman art, would suggest that the muscle cuirass was of common use among the Scholae Palatinae and Protectores units. Since the days of the Praetorians, the muscle cuirass had been the favourite kind of personal protection for all the Roman "guard" corps; apparently, this general trend continued during the late Empire.

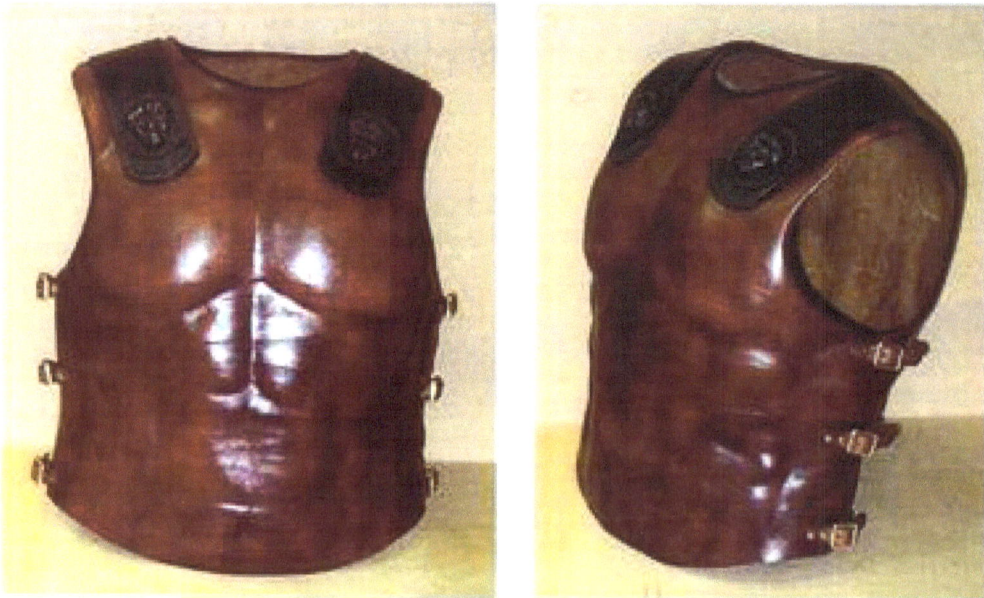

Fig 46. An example of a muscle cuirass

Fig 47. Legionary of the Matiarii seniores, wearing a fantastic example of lorica hamata. Under the cuirass you can see the subarmalis, a leather garment worn under the armour to protect clothing and body from chafing and soiling. The Matiarii seniores were one of the legiones palatinae under command of the magister militum praesentalis II in the eastern Empire. The name Matiarii might have something to do with Mars directly, but it is more likely to have come by an indirect route, from mattiobarbuli (also known as plumbatae). It is thus very probable that the units having this denomination were armed with darts. (Giuseppe Rava)

Shields

By the end of the 3rd century the traditional rectangular scutum started to disappear. Fourth century archaeological finds (especially from the fortress of Dura Europos) indicate the subsequent general use of oval or round shields, which were not semi-cylindrical but either dished (bowl-shaped) or flat. Roman artwork from the end of the 3rd century until the end of the western Empire shows the troops with oval or round shields. The new oval shield was not only much larger than the previous model, but almost flat instead of being laterally curved. It was made of solid planks instead of plywood and was supported by a double grip at elbow and hand (the old scutum had a single central grip). The oval scutum was about 110cm high and 90cm wide, constructed with 1cm thick wood planks. It was covered and bound with leather. A hollow boss, could be iron or bronze, covered the central hand grip.

As previously mentioned, for logistical reasons, the late Roman soldiers were not issued standard equipment but were only given an allowance to buy their own clothing and equipment; this may or may not have included shields. In order to achieve some kind of uniformity on the field of battle, the soldiers of each unit had the same emblem painted on their shields. The "*Notitia Dignitatum*" contains most of the shield emblems used during the late Roman period (see the specific section devoted to the Notitia in this book); however, the shields of some categories of troops are not represented: none of the limitanei are illustrated, nor (with some exceptions) are those of the eastern cavalry units. Why these units are omitted is still a mystery; perhaps they were included in the original, but not reported in the surviving copies we have today. It is clear that, for practical reasons, the shields effectively used on campaign would not maintain the perfect emblems like those painted in the "*Notitia Dignitatum*". After a battle or a long march, damaged shields would have had to be replaced from battlefield salvage or perharps from a central reserve, so it is highly unlikely that a soldier on campaign would have had the time or the paint to reproduce the highly detailed designs shown in the "*Notitia Dignitatum*" before his next engagement. At best, he might have managed to put a quick and simple coat of paint in the official colour of his unit. The variety of symbols and colours, mixed in a multitude of combinations, that appears in the "Notitia" is simply astonishing: for this reason, it is very hard to believe that each soldier of each unit respected such a complex system of shield emblems.

Fig 48. Eastern Warrior God painted on a shield found at Dura Europos

Fig 49. An example of a wooden Shield missing central boss

Swords

From the late 2nd to the early 3rd century, the earlier Roman gladius was gradually replaced by the spatha. This was introduced to the Roman Army in the early Imperial period, by Celtic cavalry auxiliaries who continued to use their Celtic long swords, with blade lengths of 60 to 85 cm. From the early 3rd century, legionaries and cavalrymen began to wear their swords on the left side, perhaps as a result of the substitution of the short gladius with the longer spatha. This was a type of straight and long sword, measuring between 0.75 and 1 m. It gradually became the standard heavy infantry sword, initially relegating the gladius to use as a light infantry weapon.

It seems that the spatha started to replace the gladius in the front ranks, in order to give the infantry more reach when thrusting; in any case, it was adopted earlier by cavalrymen. While the infantry version had a long point, those carried by the cavalry had a rounded tip that prevented accidental stabbing of the cavalryman's foot. Archaeological evidence of spatha has been found in Britain and Germany, indicating its widespread use during this period. The spatha remained popular throughout the Migration Period, serving as a model for the famous Viking swords. It later evolved into the knightly sword of the High Middle Ages.

Fig 52. Reproduction spatha and scabbard (Odin Blades)

Fig 53. Late Roman scabbard binding

Fig 50. & 51. Examples of spatha blades

Polearms and Throwing Weapons

Since the days of the Republic, the Roman legionary's fighting style was defined by two weapons: the pilum and the gladius. The pilum was a javelin with a long iron shank for punching through enemy shields and armour, usually thrown at close range. The legionary would then draw his gladius to charge into the enemy. The infantryman of the late Imperial period fought more or less in the same way, but his sword was by now much longer (albeit remaining a cut-and-thrust weapon). Instead of the pilum, the late legionary could use one of a vast selection of javelins to break up the ranks of the enemy: from new and heavier pila to long-shanked spicula with barbed heads, or small plumbata darts with lead weights. Butt-spikes protected the base of the shaft of the spear or javelin from rot and could be used as a secondary weapon.

The spiculum was the late Roman spear that replaced the pilum as the infantryman's main throwing javelin around 250 AD. Some scholars have theorized that it could have resulted from the gradual combination of the pilum with Germanic javelins, known as angon or bebra. The angon was similar to (and probably derived from) the pilum, having a barbed head and a long narrow socket or shank, made of iron mounted on a wooden haft. The barbs were designed to lodge in the opponent's shield so that it could not be removed. The long iron shank prevented the head from being cut from the shaft. The angon was likely designed for the purpose of disabling enemy shields, thus leaving combatants vulnerable and disrupting enemy formations. The shaft may have been decorated and iron or bronze rings were sometimes fitted onto it, which may have marked the center of balance and thus the best place to hold the weapon.

Fig 54. Spiculum

The spiculum was better than the old pilum when used as a thrusting spear, but still maintained some of the former weapon's penetrative power when thrown. The main difference between the spiculum and the pilum was the length of the thin point, because the spiculum tended to have a much shorter iron point. It is believed to have been shorter than its ancestor, perhaps being 190 cm long. The exact design of the spiculum is not fully known, as many variants have been found in digs. Vegetius mentions the spiculum in his military manual, but some scholars still believe that it was simply a later name for the pilum. Whatever the case, most historians accept that the spiculum evolved from the earlier javelins used by the Roman Army.

The spiculum was usually combined with a lighter and longer ranged javelin called the verutum. This javelin had been used for skirmishing purposes since the days of the Republican velites (light infantrymen), in combination with the heavier pilum. The verutum's shaft was about 1.1 meters long, so much shorter than that of the pilum, and its point measured about 13 centimeters long. The verutum had either an iron shank like the pilum or a tapering metal head. It had a narrow armour-piercing head similar to that of the larger weapons, though obviously with nothing like the same chance of penetrating. Possibly because of the new emphasis on long range fighting, the spiculum seems to have gone out of use at the end of the 4th century AD, while the verutum remained in use until the end of the western Empire.

Plumbatae or martiobarbuli were lead-weighted darts, usually carried by the heavy infantrymen on the back of their shields. The best written source we have for these tactical weapons is Vegetius' "De Re Militari":

"...The exercise of the loaded javelins, called martiobarbuli, must not be omitted. We formerly had two legions in Illyricum, consisting of six thousand men each, which from their extraordinary dexterity and skill in the use of these weapons were distinguished by the same appellation. They supported for a long time the weight of all the wars and distinguished themselves so remarkably that the Emperors Diocletian and Maximian on their accession honoured them with the titles of Jovian and Herculean and preferred them before all the other legions. Every soldier carries five of these javelins in the hollow of his shield. And thus the legionary soldiers seem to supply the place of archers, for they wound both the men and horses of the enemy before they come within reach of the common missile weapons..."

Fig 55. Spiculum spear heads

Fig 56. Examples of Late Roman spearheads

Fig 57. Martiobarbuli

Fig 58. Plumbatae

These projectiles were initially introduced into two Legiones Palatinae, the Ioviani and Herculiani that were raised by Diocletian; later they spread to the other legions and auxilia. A second source, also from the late 4th century, is an anonymous treatise titled "De Rebus Bellicis", which briefly discusses (so far archaeologically unattested) "spiked plumbatae" (plumbata tribolata), but which is also the only source that shows an image of what a plumbata looked like. The image shows a short arrow with a weight attached to the shaft. Although only later copies of the original manuscript exist, this is confirmed by the remains which have so far turned up in the archaeological digs. The term plumbatae comes from the word plumbum, or lead, and can be translated as "lead-weighted darts". Martiobarbuli is most likely an assimilation of "Martio-barbuli", which means "little barbs of Mars". The barb implied a barbed head and Mars was the god of war. Archaeology gives us a clearer picture of the plumbatae. One relic found in England and identified as the head of a plumbata is a fletched dart with an iron head, weighted with lead. The modern reconstructions seem entirely consistent with Vegetius' description. While the plumbatae had little armor penetrating power, their barbed heads made them very suitable for crippling an unarmored man or animal. At the same time they could outrange conventional javelins.

The late Roman heavy cavalry was mainly armed with the contus (or kontos): this was a type of long wooden lance used by Iranian cavalry, most notably cataphracts. The term "contus" was originally used to describe Sarmatian long spears developed in the early to mid 1st century AD, from shorter spear-type weapons. The contus was used at the Battle of Carrhae, by Parthian cataphracts, in conjunction with light horse archers, who annihilated a Roman force of over three times their numbers. As shown by contemporary artwork, the contus was about 4 metres long, though longer examples may have existed: later Parthian and Sassanian clibanarii reportedly used conti of longer lengths. Because of its length it had to be wielded with two hands while directing the horse using the knees, which required a lot of training and good horsemanship to use.

The contus was reputedly a weapon of great power, especially if compared to other cavalry weapons of its time. It was described by Plutarch as being "heavy with steel" and capable of impaling two men at once. Its length was probably the origin of its name, as the Greek word kontos could also mean "oar" or "barge-pole". The Roman cavalry introduced the contus on a large scale after facing the Sarmatian heavy cavalry. The wealthiest Sarmatian warriors were well armoured with iron helmets and body armour and used the contus in a very effective way. After seeing the success of Sarmatian heavy cavalry tactics and equipment, the Romans decided to adopt them for their own heavy mounted units. As a result, they started to deploy both native and mercenary units of cataphracts throughout the Empire, from Asia Minor all the way to Britain, where a contingent of 5,500 Sarmatian cataphracts was posted in the 3rd century by Emperor Marcus Aurelius.

Fig 59. Late Roman spear tips

Bows

The early Romans had very few archers, if any. As their Empire grew, they started to recruit mercenary or auxiliary archers from other nations, especially from Crete and the Levant. The Romans had always been pragmatic in adapting foreign military techniques from their enemies. As a result, they quickly adopted the compact power of the composite bow for use in the army. By the 4th century, archers with powerful composite bows were a regular part of Roman armies throughout the Empire, especially in the eastern half.

The normal weapon of late Roman archers, both infantry and cavalry units, was the composite bow, although Vegetius recommends training recruits with the arcubus ligneis (wooden bow), which may have been made in the northern European longbow tradition. According to Vegetius:

> "...A third or fourth of the youngest and fittest soldiers should also be exercised at the post with bows and arrows made for that purpose only. The masters for this branch must be chosen with care and must apply themselves diligently to teach the men to hold the bow in a proper position, to bend it with strength, to keep the left hand steady, to draw the right with skill, to direct both the attention and the eye to the object, and to take their aim with equal certainty either on foot or on horseback. But this is not to be acquired without great application, nor to be retained without daily exercise and practice..."

Apparently, the simpler and traditional longbows were still used in the west also on the field of battle. Crafting a composite bow may take a week's work, plus a drying time of some months; a longbow could be made in a day and dried in a week. Historically, peoples living in humid or rainy regions have favoured wooden bows, while those living in dry or arid regions have favoured composite ones.

A composite bow is made from horn, wood and sinew laminated together. The horn is on the belly facing the archer, while sinew is on the outer side of a wooden core. When the bow is drawn, the sinew (stretched on the outside) and horn (compressed on the inside) store more energy than wood for the same length of bow. The strength can be made similar to that of all-wood bows, with similar draw-length and therefore a similar amount of energy delivered to the arrow, but from a much shorter bow. The construction of a composite bow was a very complex process: it required more varieties of material than a wooden bow and much more time. The wooden core gives the bow its shape and dimensional stability. It was often made of multiple pieces, joined with animal glue in V-splices, so the wood must accept glue well.

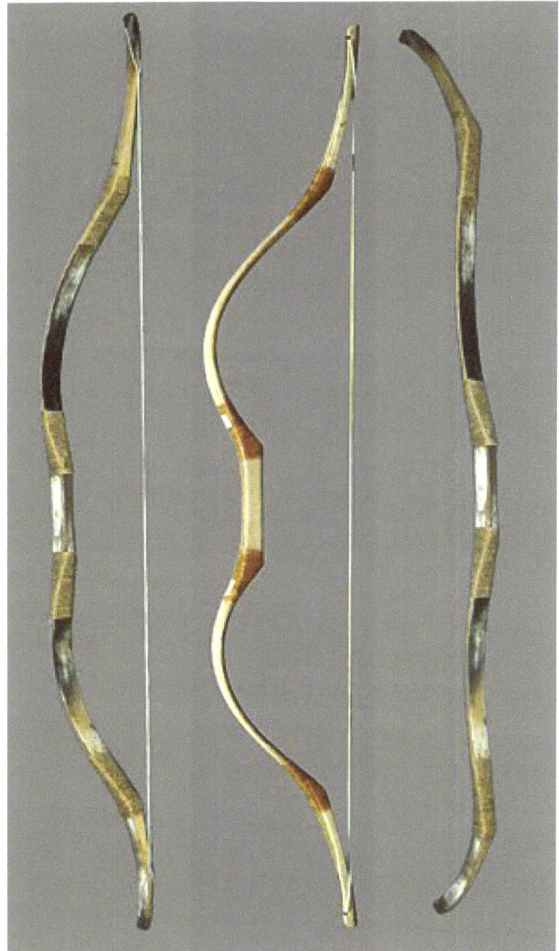

Fig 60. Examples of Hunnic composite bows

Pieced construction allows the sharp bends that many designs require and the use of woods with different mechanical properties for the bending and nonbending sections. In fact, the wood of the bending part of the limb must endure intense shearing stress. A thin layer of horn was glued onto what would be the belly of the bow; this could store more energy than wood in compression. Goat and sheep horn was commonly used for this purpose. The sinew, soaked in animal glue, was then laid in layers on the back of the bow; the strands of sinew were oriented along the length of the bow. The sinew was normally obtained from the lower legs and back of wild deer or domestic ungulates. Sinew would extend farther than wood, again allowing more energy storage. Hide glue was used to attach layers of sinew to the back of the bow and to attach the horn belly to the wooden core. The animal glue used could lose strength in humid conditions and be quickly ruined by submersion or rain: for this reason, the "Strategikon" (a famous 6th-century Byzantine military manual) advised the horse archers of the Byzantine Army to store their bows in protective leather cases in order to keep them dry. After some months of drying the bow was finally ready for use.

The main advantage of composite bows over longbows (made from a single piece of wood) is their combination of smaller size with high power. They are therefore more convenient than longbows when the archer is mobile, as from horseback. Almost all composite bows are also recurve ones, as the shape curves away from the archer; this design gives higher draw-weight in the early stages of the archer's draw, storing somewhat more total energy for a given final draw-weight. It would be possible to make a wooden bow that has the same shape, length and draw-weight of a composite bow, but it could not store the energy and would break before full draw. However, for most practical non-mounted archery purposes, composite construction offers no particular advantages: this could explain why the use of wooden longbows survived during the late Roman period.

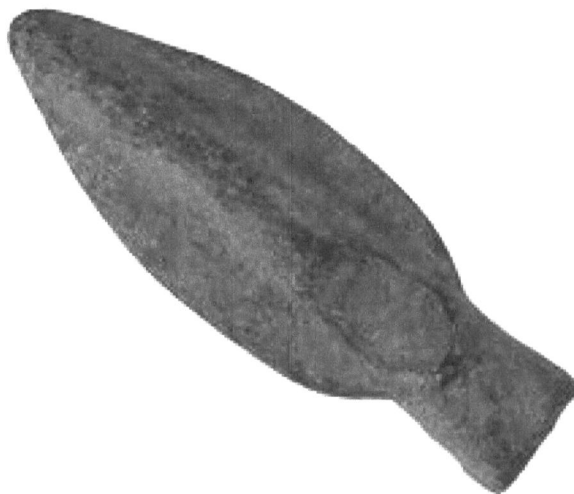

Fig 61. A Late Roman arrowhead

Sagittarii was the Latin term for archers. By the 5th century, there were numerous Roman cavalry regiments trained to use the bow as a supplement to their swords and lances, but the sagittarii appeared to have used the bow as their primary rather than supplemental weapon. According to the "Notitia Dignitatum" most units of sagittarii, especially of equites sagittarii (mounted archers), were located in the eastern Empire or in Africa. Possibly some of the other cavalry regiments also carried bows as back-up weapons, but were not the dedicated mounted archers that the sagittarii were. The use of bows as a primary cavalry weapon originated in the eastern Empire in the later 4th and earlier 5th centuries, to help the Roman Army counter Persian and Hunnic bow-armed cavalry. By the time of the "Strategikon" and of Procopius' histories, the main effective arm of Roman armies was cavalry and the majority of cavalrymen were armed with bows. After the fall of the western Empire, eastern Roman armies maintained their tradition of horse archery for centuries. The method used by cavalry to carry arrows also showed clear nomadic influence, because they were held point upwards in a barrel quiver hung from the belt. Infantry quivers, instead, were round-bottomed cylinders hanging from a shoulder-strap, which hold the arrows point downwards. In either case a man normally carried 30 to 40 arrows at a time.

Fig 62. Gothic archer, armed with the traditional wooden longbow of northern Europe. (Giuseppe Rava)

HIGH COMMAND STRUCTURE OF THE EAST ROMAN ARMY (ca. 395 AD)

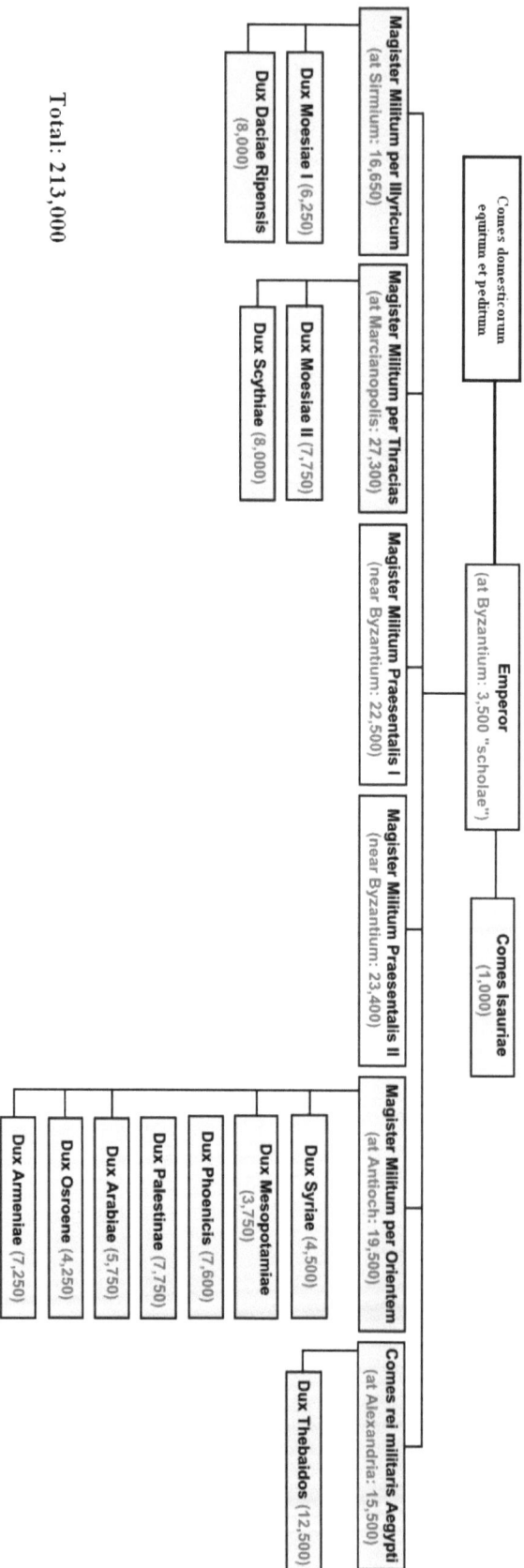

Emperor
(at Byzantium: 3,500 "scholae")

Comes domesticorum
equitum et peditum

Comes Isauriae
(1,000)

Magister Militum per Illyricum
(at Sirmium: 16,650)

Dux Moesiae I (6,250)

Dux Daciae Ripensis
(8,000)

Magister Militum per Thracias
(at Marcianopolis: 27,300)

Dux Moesiae II (7,750)

Dux Scythiae (8,000)

Magister Militum Praesentalis I
(near Byzantium: 22,500)

Magister Militum Praesentalis II
(near Byzantium: 23,400)

Magister Militum per Orientem
(at Antioch: 19,500)

Dux Syriae (4,500)

Dux Mesopotamiae
(3,750)

Dux Phoenicis (7,600)

Dux Palestinae (7,750)

Dux Arabiae (5,750)

Dux Osroene (4,250)

Dux Armeniae (7,250)

Comes rei militaris Aegypti
(at Alexandria: 15,500)

Dux Thebaidos (12,500)

Total: 213,000

HIGH COMMAND STRUCTURE OF THE WEST ROMAN ARMY (ca. 410 AD)

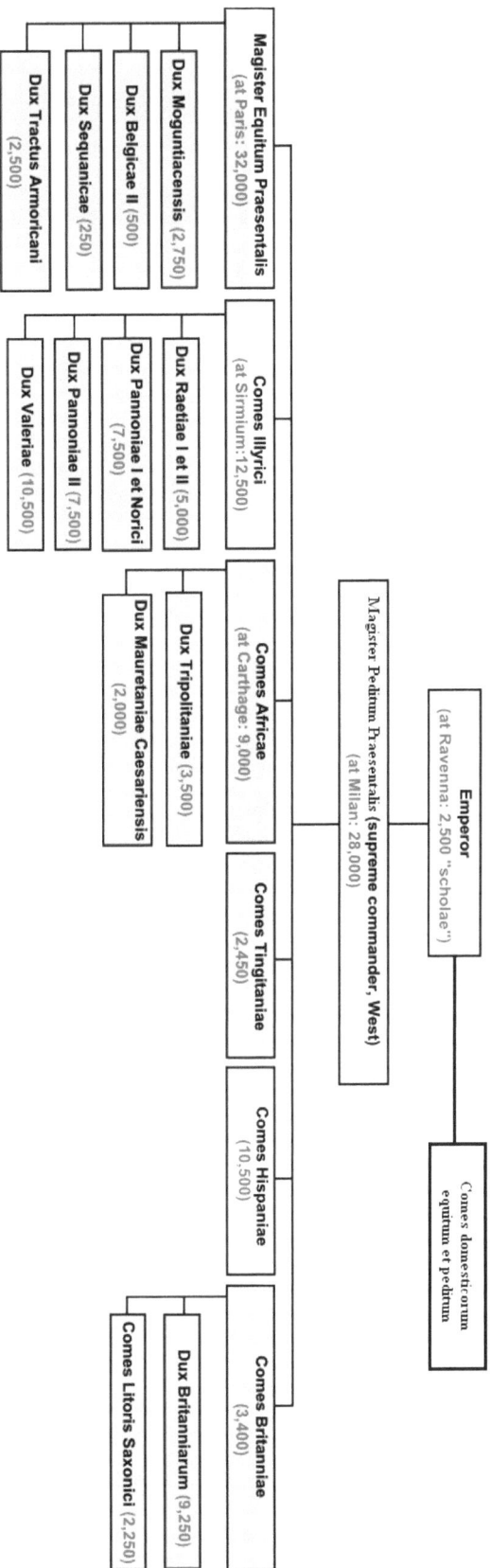

Emperor
(at Ravenna: 2,500 "scholae")

Comes domesticorum
equitum et peditum

Magister Peditum Praesentalis (supreme commander, West)
(at Milan: 28,000)

Magister Equitum Praesentalis
(at Paris: 32,000)

- **Dux Moguntiacensis** (2,750)
- **Dux Belgicae II** (500)
- **Dux Sequanicae** (250)
- **Dux Tractus Armoricani** (2,500)

Comes Illyrici
(at Sirmium: 12,500)

- **Dux Raetiae I et II** (5,000)
- **Dux Pannoniae I et Norici** (7,500)
- **Dux Pannoniae II** (7,500)
- **Dux Valeriae** (10,500)

Comes Africae
(at Carthage: 9,000)

- **Dux Tripolitaniae** (3,500)
- **Dux Mauretaniae Caesariensis** (2,000)

Comes Tingitaniae
(2,450)

Comes Hispaniae
(10,500)

Comes Britanniae
(3,400)

- **Dux Britanniarum** (9,250)
- **Comes Litoris Saxonici** (2,250)

Total: 154,000

Plate A: Late Roman officers

A1: Officer of the Brachiati iuniores, 410 AD

The Brachiati iuniores were an auxilia palatina unit, under command of the magister militum praesentalis I in the eastern Empire. The name Brachiati is usually taken to refer to upper arm bracelets (bracchia) or trousers (brachae), and is shared with five other units in the Notitia. This officer has a ridge helmet of the "Berkasovo-type", found at Deurne in the Netherlands. It is covered in silver-gilt sheathing and has very rich decorations. As many high officers, he is wearing a simple muscle cuirass used in combination with white leather "pteruges". Note the large purple oval patches decorating his brown cloak.

A2: Officer of the Celtae seniores, 420 AD

The Celtae seniores were an auxilia palatina unit, under command of the magister peditum praesentalis in Italy. Our officer is wearing the pileus pannonicus ("Pannonian cap"), a kind of headgear very popular during the late Roman period. This pillbox cap first appeared in the 2nd century AD and had become all the rage by the 4th century, eventually disappearing in the 6th. It was made of leather or felt, being frequently covered with fur (like in this case). The officer has a tunica manicata with rich decorations, including clavii (decorative stripes) and orbiculi (decorative patches). Yellow tunics are portrayed only on officers, likely because Saffron was an expensive dye.

A3: Officer of the Comites Alani, 415 AD

The Comites Alani were one of the vexillationes palatinae under command of the magister peditum praesentalis in Italy. They were likely recruited, at least initially, from Alans settled in Gaul. This officer is wearing the equipment of a light cavalry unit, with no armour. He has a Spangenhelm with nasal and wears a tunic with clavii and orbiculi in various colours. In addition to his spatha, he has a long stick; this was a symbol of command in the Roman Army, since the days of the vine-sticks carried by centurions.

A4: Officer of the Equites Honoriani seniores, 410 AD

The Equites Honoriani seniores were one of the vexillationes comitatenses under command of the magister equitum praesentalis in Gaul. The name Honoriani refers to the Emperor Honorius, who succeeded his father Theodosius I in 395 AD, around the time the Notitia was first compiled. The presence of large numbers of units named after Honorius in the western half of the Notitia, compared to very few in the east, is one of the clearest indications that the eastern portion was not amended much, or even at all, after the death of Theodosius, while the western portion was extensively updated during the first two decades of the 5th century. The ridge helmet, of the "Berkasovo-type", is made of iron and sheathed in silver-gilt. It is richly decorated with glass gems. This particular helmet is from the so-called "Berkasovo treasure" of Novi Sad, in Serbia. In addition, the officer has a cloak made with fur (very popular in the northern regions of western Europe) and a lorica squamata of excellent quality.

Plate B: Guard units

B1: Guardsman of the Germani Corporis Custodes, 400 AD
This Germanic soldier is clearly dressed for palace duty. The kind of clothing that he is wearing gives a good idea of the high level of complexity reached by dress decorations during the last centuries of the Roman Empire. Examples of highly decorative military clothing have been found on late Roman mosaics, bas-reliefs, plates and manuscripts. Guard units, in particular, had very ornate garments similar to those worn by high ranking officers. Note also the magnificent sword, having a red scabbard with decorative fittings. Around the neck of this soldier you can see a "torc": this was a large and rigid (or at least stiff) neck ring in metal, made either as a single piece or from strands twisted together. The great majority were open at the front, although some had hook and ring closures. Many seem designed for near-permanent wear and would have been difficult to remove. For the Iron Age Celts the gold torc seems to have been a key object, identifying the wearer as a person of high rank; many of the finest works of ancient Celtic art are torcs. However, torc styles of neck-ring are found as part of the jewellery styles of various other cultures and periods, including the Germanic tribes of late Antiquity.

B2: Naval officer of the Classis Germanica, 355-359 AD
The Classis Germanica was the Roman fleet which controlled the Rhine and its relative frontier. Due to the Third Century Crisis, it was reduced in size and lost much of its power; however, at the beginning of the fourth century, it was reorganized by Emperor Constantine. During the following decades the Classis Germanica played again a very important role in the defence of the Rhine frontier, taking part to the campaigns of Julian against the invading Franks and Alemanni (355-359 AD). By the end of the fifth century it was no longer in existence: in fact, it is not even mentioned in the "Notitia Dignitatum". This naval officer has a ridge helmet of the "Intercisa-type", known as "Augsburg-Pfersee Helmet". The magnificent muscle cuirass is used in combination with "pteruges" and shows protective lappets around the lower abdomen. According to Vegetius, the late Roman marines and sailors were usually dressed in venetus, a kind of sea-blue which was their peculiar colour. The cloak of this officer, albeit being in venetus, is of mixed Romano-Germanic style (see the decorations); this was something quite common for units deployed on the frontier, especially for limitanei.

B3: Bucellarius in Papal service, 470 AD
Germanic soldiers were part of the Papal retinue during the last decades of the western Empire, acting as his personal guardsmen. This figure is based on the "Judgement of Solomon" fresco of Santa Maria Lata, in Rome. The tunic of this bucellarius is of very good quality, being made of wool and linen. The leather greaves, having red decorations, are copied from some mosaics of this period. Note the rich decorative elements placed on the shield, even on the boss.

B4: Hun of Flavius Aetius' bodyguard, 435 AD
Flavius Aetius, the greatest Roman general of the late Empire, was protected by Hun bodyguards who were extremely loyal to him. As a boy, he spent many years with the Huns as a hostage, thus learning their culture and military traditions. He had a very good relationship with the Huns also during the following years, forming an alliance with them in 433-439, with the objective of defending Gaul from the Germanic invasions. In 451 AD, when Attila decided to invade the western Empire, Aetius was able to defeat his ex-allies at the decisive battle of the Catalaunian Plains. Aetius, as supreme commander of the western military forces, was not a normal magnate who could afford some bucellarii: this is clear from the fantastic dress worn by this Hun. In particular, note the design of the decorative elements (clavii and orbiculi) and the magnificent manufacture of the sword and knife. The skull of the Huns was deliberately constricted with fabric bandages from infancy, so that it grew excessively tall and conical.

Plate C: Cataphractii and Clibanarii

C1: Clibanarius of the eastern Empire's Domestici Equites, 420 AD

The Clibanarii were the eastern equivalent of the cataphracts, having more or less their same equipment. This kind of heavy cavalry was originally employed by the Sassanid Persians and later adopted by the eastern Roman armies. Later clibanarii tended to have half armoured horses like this, instead of fully armoured ones. In the hot regions of the Middle East, cladding the horse with full armour would increase the risk of overheating due to poor ventilation, not to mention the extra weight. For these reasons having only the front of the horse armoured was a good compromise. The western cataphracts, instead, always had horses with full armour. Because of their heavy protections, clibanarii and cataphractii had no shields or very small and round ones, like those represented in the plate. These were usually strapped to the forearm and used as a protection against arrows directed to the head of the horseman. Our Clibanarius is from the eastern Domestici Equites, the mounted bodyguard of the Emperor. It is reasonable to suppose that - as an elite cavalry unit - the Domestici Equites were equipped as heavy cavalry both in the western and eastern Empire. This soldier carries a segmented Spangenhelm of Italo-Germanic form, together with a lamellar cuirass. This kind of body armour was introduced very late in the Roman armies, as a result of the increasing Turco-Central Asian military influence. Apparently, lamellar armour was used extensively only by the heavy cavalry (both clibanarii and cataphractii). Obviously, the horse has the same kind of armour. Note the rich decorations on the front of the saddle and on the tunic.

C2: Cataphractus of the western Empire's Domestici Equites, 410 AD

This mounted bodyguard of the western Emperor has the perfect equipment of a heavy cavalry cataphract. The helmet is a Spangenhelm found at Deir el-Medina in Egypt; its main features include the peculiar neck protection and cheek flaps. The armour is an excellent combination of lamellar armour (protecting the torso), segmented armour and lorica hamata. The saddle and armour of the horse are of excellent quality: note the decorated protections for the horse's eyes.

C3: Cataphractus of the Equites Honoriani Taifali iuniores, 395 AD

The Equites Honoriani Taifali iuniores were one of the vexillationes comitatenses under command of the Comes Britanniae. The term Taifali comes from a tribal name first recorded in the mid-3rd century AD, although whether the Taifali were of Germanic or Sarmatian ethnicity is debated. They fought in many conflicts during the 4th century both for and against Rome, being famous for their heavy cavalry. Various units incorporating the name Taifali are listed in the Notitia; this one, in particular, was probably formed with Taifali prisoners during the reign of Emperor Honorius. It was one of the most important cavalry units stationed in Britain. Because of the Taifali's long tradition as heavy cavalrymen, it is reasonable to suppose that the soldiers from this unit were equipped as cataphracts. Our soldier has a cavalry helmet with moulded facemask: these kinds of helmet were initially worn only during parades and hippika gymnasia (ritual displays or tournaments performed by the Roman cavalry since the early days of the Empire), thus being known as "sports helmets". Later they started to be employed also on the field of battle, particularly by the cataphracts who appreciated them for the mask protecting face. Helmets with facemasks were commonly used also by the Sassanid heavy cavalry. Obviously they lost most of the decorations which were typical of the early "parade" models. The armour is a combination of lorica hamata, lorica squamata and segmented armour. Note the magnificent chanfron, used to protect the horse's head.

Plate D: Late Roman legionaries

D1: Legionary of the Quinta Macedonica, 395 AD

The Quinta Macedonica was one of the oldest Roman legions, having been originally levied in 43 BC. In the "Notitia Dignitatum" it is listed as one of the legiones comitatenses under command of the magister militum per Orientem. In addition, it had two detachments: one in Egypt (under command of the Comes limitis Aegypti) and the other in Dacia (under command of the Dux Daciae ripensis). It was active until the conquest of Egypt by the Arabs in 637. This makes Legio V Macedonica the longest lived Roman legion, spanning 680 years from 43 BC to 637 AD. This legionary has a Spangenhelm and a bronze lorica squamata, very popular in the eastern half of the Empire. He is using one of the five plumbatae that were usually carried on the back of the shield.

D2: Legionary of the Herculiani seniores, 475 AD

The Herculiani, together with the Ioviani, were formed by Emperor Diocletian after the end of the Third Century Crisis: the former from the Legio VI Herculia and the latter from the Legio V Iovia. It is said that Diocletian formed these new legiones palatinae with the intention of using them to replace the Praetorian Guard (something he was finally unable to do). In any case, these two legions from Illyricum were elite units since their foundation: Diocletian himself was from Illyricum, so he was absolutely sure of these units' loyalty. Diocletian and Maximian even honoured them with the titles of Herculiani and Ioviani: in fact, Hercules was the god protector of Diocletian and Iuppiter the god protector of Maximian. As we have already seen, they were also the first legions to employ the new plumbatae in a very effective way. With the division of the Roman Empire, the Herculiani and Ioviani were both divided in seniores and iuniores. The Herculiani seniores are listed in the Notitia as one of the legiones palatinae under command of the magister peditum praesentalis in Italy. The soldier wears an Attic-style helmet, a model that was less popular than the Spangenhelm or ridge helmet but which had a certain diffusion during the very last decades of the western Empire. In addition, he has an excellent lorica hamata.

D3: Legionary of the Secunda Britannica, 410 AD

The Secunda Britannica was one of the legiones comitatenses under command of the magister equitum praesentalis in Gaul. Part, at least, of this unit served on the Saxon Shore of Britain until the Roman withdrawal from the island. Some scholars have suggested that its title may indicate the last "descendants" of the old Legio II Augusta, one of the original garrison legions of Britain. The ridge helmet of this legionary is of the so-called "Intercisa IV-type", with its typical crest. Many modern reconstructions show the shafts of late Roman spears painted with bright colours: personally, I think that we have not enough primary sources to consider painted shafts as an item of common use on the battlefield. It is much more probable that spears with painted shafts were used only during parades or cavalry hippika gymnasia.

D4: Legionary of the Cornuti seniores, 420 AD

The name Cornuti is usually taken to mean "the horned ones", also because their shield emblem seems to show a pair of horns. The original Cornuti are believed to have been one of the foremost components of Constantine's army when he defeated Maxentius in 312 AD, since scholars have identified some of the figures shown on the Arch of Constantine as being soldiers of the Cornuti, due to their helmet decorations looking like horns. According to Ammianus, the Cornuti were typically brigaded with the Brachiati and the two units were famous for their rendition of the barritus (war-cry). When the unit was divided between seniores and iuniores is unknown; in any case, the Cornuti iuniores of the eastern Empire took part to the battle of Adrianople. In the Notitia, the Cornuti seniores are listed as one of the auxilia palatina units under command of the magister peditum praesentalis in Italy. The figure wears a plumed version of the ridge helmet: it has been suggested by some scholars that plumes usually matched shield colours, in order to help unit identification on the battlefield. The armour is a lorica hamata.

Plate E: Late Roman light troops

E1: Archer, 400 AD

This was the typical appearance of a common late Roman archer. Apparently, the pileus pannonicus was the standard headgear for light troops, which usually carried no helmet even in battle. This soldier is armed with the traditional wooden longbow of western Europe, plus a spatha as secondary weapon. The white tunic has the usual decorative clavii and orbiculi.

E2: Light cavalryman of the Equites Mauri feroces, 410 AD

The Equites Mauri feroces were one of the vexillationes comitatenses under command of the magister peditum praesentalis in Italy. The name Mauri denotes the Moorish peoples, although there is indication that by this date the term, as used in the Roman military, denoted not an ethnicity but a particular kind of military unit. Possibly a light unit, whether of foot or, as in this case, of horse, because that is how Moors fought when the Romans first encountered them. In fact, Moors were famous for being excellent light cavalrymen since the days of the Punic Wars. The term feroces means "ferocious", but despite being a good name for a military unit it is not a common one in the Notitia. The soldier is armed with a sword and a couple of short javelins (of the verutum type). Note the peculiar hair style, a distinctive feature of Moors and Numidians.

E3: Slinger, 400 AD

For most of the early Empire, the Romans employed mercenary Balearic slingers; by the time of the late Empire, however, the sling became one of the standard weapons for Roman missile troops. According to Vegetius: "...Recruits are to be taught the art of throwing stones both with the hand and sling. The inhabitants of the Balearic Islands are said to have been the inventors of slings, and to have managed them with surprising dexterity, owing to the manner of bringing up their children. The children were not allowed to have their food by their mothers till they had first struck it with their sling. Soldiers, notwithstanding their defensive armour, are often more annoyed by the round stones from the sling than by all the arrows of the enemy. Stones kill without mangling the body, and the contusion is mortal without loss of blood. It is universally known that the ancients employed slingers in all their engagements. There is the greater reason for instructing all troops, without exception, in this exercise, as the sling cannot be reckoned any encumbrance, and often is of the greatest service, especially when they are obliged to engage in stony places, to defend a mountain or an eminence, or to repulse an enemy at the attack of a fortress or city...". Instead of the traditional sling employed by Balearic slingers, late Roman soldier were equipped with the so-called "staff sling": this consisted of a staff (a length of wood) with a short sling at one end. One cord of the sling was firmly attached to the staff, while the other end had a loop that could slide off and release the projectile. Staff slings were extremely powerful, because the staff could be made as long as two meters, creating a powerful lever. Ancient art shows slingers holding staff slings by one end, with the pocket behind them, and using both hands to throw the staves forward over their heads. The staff sling could throw heavy projectiles at much greater distance and at a higher arc than a traditional shepherd's hand sling and could be as accurate in practiced hands. Our slinger wears the usual pileus pannonicus and a white tunic, this time with blue clavii and orbiculi.

E4: Eastern archer, 450 AD

Since the mid-Republic, the archers of the Roman Army were virtually all mercenaries from the island of Crete, which boasted a long specialist tradition for archers. During the late-Republic and the early Empire, Cretans were gradually eclipsed by men from other (much more populous) regions with strong archery traditions subjugated by the Romans. These included Thrace, Anatolia and, above all, Syria. Of 32 sagittarii units attested in the mid-2nd century, 13 had Syrian names, 7 Thracian, 5 were from Anatolia, 1 from Crete and the remaining 6 were of uncertain origin. In fact, three distinct types of archers are shown on Trajan's Column: with scalar cuirass, conical steel helmet and cloak; without armour, with cloth conical cap and long tunic; or equipped in the same way as general auxiliary foot-soldiers. The first type were the Syrian and Anatolian units of archers; the second type were the Thracians; the third type are of uncertain origin (probably Romans). During the late Empire, in addition to auxilia from the eastern provinces, the Romans also employed large numbers of mercenary or allied archers from the small client states of the Middle East. Our soldier has the usual equipment of the Levantine auxiliary or mercenary archers who served the Roman Empire: the cloak and the lorica squamata are more or less the same shown on Trajan's Column, while the helmet and weapons are completely different. The conical helmet has been replaced by a Spangenhelm of Sassanian pattern; the magnificent sword and knife are also of Sassanian origins. The main weapon is a recurved composite bow: a sophisticated, compact and powerful weapon.

Plate F: The Rhine frontier

F1: Frankish warrior, 475 AD

This Frankish warrior could be either a laetus from the Franci or an enemy of the Empire. He carries the usual heavy equipment of rich Germanic warriors, with a chain mail protecting the upper part of the body. The magnificent Spangenhelm is from Krefeld-Gellep: the elaborate decorations on its panels suggest Italian manufacture. The shield, as common practice for Germanic warriors of the time, is decorated with a combination of metal plaques and bolt heads. In addition to the sword and angon, this warrior carries also a small knife and a seax (also known as scramasax): this was one of the most characteristic weapons used by Germanic warriors, being a sort of iron dagger with a single cutting edge and a long tapering point.

F2: Legionary of the Germaniciani iuniores, 420 AD

The Germaniciani iuniores were one of the legiones comitatenses under command of the magister peditum praesentalis in Italy. The name Germaniciani simply means "from Germany"; presumably this unit was either recruited there or served in Germany before joining the field army. The equipment of this soldier is quite simple, including a spatha and a plumed version of the ridge helmet. Note that the colour of the plume matches with red of the shield emblem.

F3: Vandal warrior, 410 AD

In 406 AD the Vandals advanced from Pannonia travelling west along the Danube; when they reached the Rhine, they met serious resistance from the Franks, who populated and controlled Romanized regions in northern Gaul. Twenty thousand Vandals died in the resulting battle against the Franks, but with the help of the Alans they finally managed to defeat the Franks and, on the last day of December of 406 AD, they crossed the Rhine (probably while it was frozen) and invaded Gaul. The Vandals devastated northern Gaul terribly, before moving southward through Aquitaine. This warrior has the usual equipment of Vandal mounted archers, influenced by the military traditions of the steppe peoples with which the Vandals came in contact during their migrations. Weaponry consists of a sword and composite bow (carried on the back, as the peculiar quiver). Our warrior wears a tunic with rich decorations around the neck and shoulders; note the high boots with knee extensions.

F4: Gallo-Roman auxiliary archer, 475 AD

The term "Gallo-Roman" describes the Romanized culture of Gaul under the rule of the Roman Empire. This was characterized by the Gaulish adoption or adaptation of Roman culture and way of life, but in a uniquely Gaulish context: for this reason, the final result was a mix of Celtic and Roman elements. This is evident also in the equipment of our archer: the checkered fabric of his cloak (a sort of "tartan") and the simple dagger are of clear Celtic origins, while the composite bow is obviously of Roman construction.

Plate G: The Danube frontier

G1: Hun horse archer, 410 AD
In 395 AD the Huns began their first large-scale attack on the eastern half of the Roman Empire. They raided Thrace, overran Armenia and pillaged Cappadocia. The Huns attacked the eastern Empire again in 408, when they crossed the Danube and captured the fortress of Castra Martis in Moesia, after which they pillaged Thrace once more. In 435 Attila and Bleda (who ruled the Huns together since the previous year) forced the eastern Empire to sign the Treaty of Margus, which gave the Huns trade rights and an annual tribute from the Romans. With their southern border protected by the terms of this treaty, the Huns could turn their full attention to the further subjugation of the Germanic tribes in the west. This Hun horse archer is performing the famous "Parthian shot", which was the basic element of the Huns' skirmishing tactics: as the archer gallops away from the enemy, he still engages him by using the technique of the backward shot. Our warrior is dressed in woollen tunic and breeches, while his jacket, leggings and cap are of goatskin. In addition to the powerful composite bow, he carries a certain number of short javelins (on the back of the saddle). The small round shield was primarily used as a protection against enemy arrows.

G2: Horse archer of the Sagittarii iuniores Orientales, 410 AD
As we have previously seen, the late Romans introduced units of horse archers in their armies as a result of the influence exerted by Persian and Hunnic bow-armed cavalry. By the time of Emperor Justinian, the units of equites sagittarii made up the largest part of the Roman Army's cavalry. The Sagittarii iuniores Orientales were one of the auxilia palatina units under command of the magister militum praesentalis II in the eastern Empire. Albeit being listed as an auxilia, it is highly probable that the soldiers of this unit were equipped as horse archers. The soldier is protected by a plumed "Attic-style" helmet and lorica squamata with red leather pteruges. This kind of helmet seems to have been particularly popular in the eastern half of the Empire: it is probable that armouries in Greek parts of the Empire continued to produce helmets which followed Hellenistic styles, with single bowl construction rather than the multi-part Spangenhelm or ridge helmet. The rest of the equipment is very similar to that of his Hun opponent, excepting the spatha: small round shield, composite bow and javelins.

G3: Heavy cavalryman of the Hiberi, 410 AD
The Hiberi were one of the auxilia palatina units under command of the magister militum praesentalis I in the eastern Empire. They were closely related to another auxilia palatina unit under command of the magister militum praesentalis II, the Thraces. Both units had a lion in their shield emblem: for this reason, they would appear to be named after peoples inhabiting mountainous regions that were in ancient times also populated by lions (the Thracians of northern Greece/southern Bulgaria and the Hiberians of the Caucasus). It is probable that the Hiberi and the Thraces were brigaded together before being split when the two parallel eastern field armies were formed. The military equipment of the Hiberians consisted of a mix of elements influenced by the various military traditions of the Caucasus: Sarmatian, Hunnic and Sassanid. In fact, we have given this soldier the equipment of a heavy cavalryman, showing a strong Sarmatian influence. The helmet is an old proto- Spangenhelm of "late Sarmatian" type, with nasal, shaped cheekpieces and a leather neckguard. The soldier is armed with a spatha and a long contus, the distinctive weapon of the Sarmatian heavy cavalry. Lorica squamata armour protects the rider and his horse.

Plate H: The Desert frontier

H1: Arab auxiliary, 300 AD
The "Notitia Dignitatum" lists three units of Arabs serving in the Roman Army: Cohors L Arabum, Cohors III felix Arabum and Ala III Arabum. Apparently, the Romans used also the term Saraceni to refer to Arabs; three units in the Notitia have this denomination: the Equites Saraceni Thamudeni, the Equites Saraceni and the Equites Saraceni indigenae. The most important Arab allies of the Empire were the Ghassanids and Tanukhids; the latter, in particular, played a key role in the defeat of Zenobia's forces by Emperor Aurelian and served as foederati (the first Arab tribe to do so). It seems that the Arabs were mostly employed as cavalrymen or mounted on camels, but in this case we have decided to represent an auxiliary light infantryman. He has the traditional Arab head-cloth called "kefiyah" and carries a Sassanian sword (presumably captured).

H2: Palmyrene heavy infantryman, 270 AD
During the Third Century Crisis, the Syrian city of Palmyra started a brief but violent period of expansionism which resulted in the formation of the short-lived "Palmyrene Empire", under the famous Queen Zenobia. The Palmyrene military forces managed to conquer Syria, Judea, Lebanon, part of Anatolia and even Egypt, before being defeated by Emperor Aurelian during the campaign of 272-273 AD. After the Roman reconquest, Palmyrene soldiers seem to have started to serve in the Roman Army; in fact, the Notitia lists two Palmyrene units: the Ala VIII Palmyrenorum and the Cuneus equitum secundorum clibanariorum Palmirenorum. This soldier is reconstructed according to the magnificent wall-paintings of Dura Europos: he wears full chain mail with integral coif and carries a large shield of reeds bound with strips of leather (used to strengthen the whole shield). The short stabbing sword is of Roman pattern.

H3: Palmyrene heavy cavalryman, 270 AD
Due to its military character and efficiency at war, Palmyra was a sort of "Sparta" among the cities of the Levant: even its gods were represented dressed in military equipment. Palmyra's army defended the city and its economy, helping to extend Palmyrene authority beyond the city walls and protecting the countryside's desert trade routes. Apparently, the city could field substantial military: Zenobia led an army of 70,000 men in the decisive Battle of Emesa. Palmyrene soldiers were recruited from the city and its territories, spanning several thousand square kilometers from the outskirts of Homs to the Euphrates valley. Non-Palmyrene soldiers were also recruited, including Nabatean cavalrymen. The Palmyrene army of the mid 3rd century AD was modelled on the Sassanids in arms and tactics. The Palmyrenes were famous archers, but the heavily armoured cavalry of the clibanarii constituted their main attacking force. Our soldier is a clibanarius from the royal guard of Palmyra: he wears heavy lamellar armour in perfect Hellenistic style, with embroidered pteruges. The tall helmet is similar to those used by Syrian auxiliary archers in Roman service.

H4: Dromedarius, 300 AD
The Romans first encountered camel-mounted troops when they fought against Seleucid King Antiochus III in 190 BC, but it was only in the 2nd century AD that a Roman camel corps was formed. In 106 AD, Trajan added to the Empire the new province of Arabia Petraea and thus created the Ala I Ulpia Dromedariorum Palmyrenorum, which was formed with camel warriors from Palmyra who had served particularly well under him. In the following decades the Romans formed various small auxilia units of dromedarii, because these proved very effective in patrolling the desert frontiers of the Empire. Their tasks included escorting convoys, defending the important routes of communication, scouting in the desert, escorting couriers and battling against desert bandits. They were organized in small squads, with special bases in the desert which provided them with food and water. It has been estimated that during the late Empire the Romans had up to a thousand of these camel-mounted soldiers, mainly recruited from Arabs. They were part of the limitanei forces stationed in the African and eastern provinces of the Empire. The dromedarius represented in our plate has a simple helmet and wears a lorica squamata with leather pteruges. In addition to the small round shield, he carries a spear and a composite bow (not visible, attached to the other side of the camel).

The Roman Army of the Notitia Dignitatum

Thanks to the Notitia Dignitatum, we are able to reconstruct considerable order of battle for both the western and eastern late Roman armies. However, we should remember that the info contained in this document dates back to 410 AD for the western Empire and 395 AD for the eastern Empire, so the two orders of battle have a different dating. The following shows the commander's title plus organization and the names of the units recognized under that command.

Eastern Roman army, 395 AD

Magister Officiorum
(commander of the Scholae Palatinae)

Schola scutariorum prima

Schola scutariorum secunda

Schola scutariorum clibanariorum

Schola scutariorum sagittariorum

Schola armaturarum iuniorum

Schola gentilium seniorum

Schola gentilium iuniorum

**Comes Domesticorum Equitum et Comes Domesticorum Peditum
(commanders of the Protectores)**

Domestici equites

Domestici pedites

**Comes Isauriae
(under direct command of the Emperor)**

Legio II Isaura

Legio III Isaura

Magister Militum Praesentalis I
(commander of the 1st central Imperial army)

Legiones Palatinae

Lanciarii seniores

Fortenses

Ioviani iuniores

Nervii

Herculiani iuniores

Matiarii iuniores

Auxilia Palatina

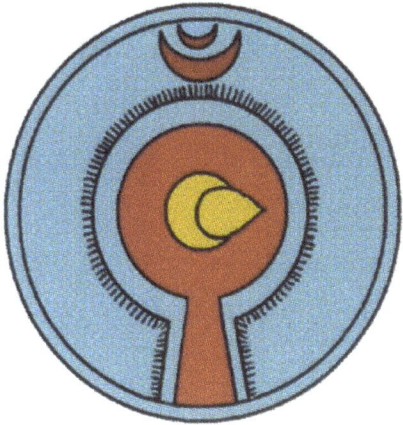

Batavi seniores

Constantiani

Brachiati iuniores

Mattiaci seniores

Salii

Sagittarii seniores Gallicani

Sagittarii iuniores Gallicani

Raetobarii

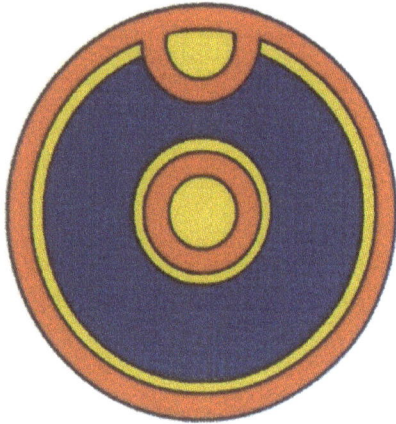

Tertii sagittarii Valentis

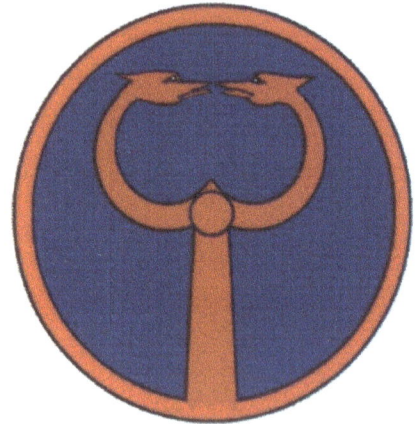

Anglevarii

Defensores

Hiberi

Visi

Primi Theodosiani

Felices Honoriani iuniores

Tertii Theodosiani

Victores

Felices Theodosiani Isauri

Vexillationes Palatinae

Equites promoti seniores
Equites Arcades
Comites clibanarii
Comites sagittarii iuniores
Comites Taifali

Vexillationes Comitatenses

Equites catafractarii Biturigenses
Equites armigeri seniores Gallicani
Equites quinto Dalmatae
Equites nono Dalmatae
Equites primi scutarii
Equites promoti iuniores
Equites primi clibanarii Parthi

Magister Militum Praesentalis II
(commander of the 2nd central Imperial army)

Legiones Palatinae

Matiarii seniores

Scythae

Daci

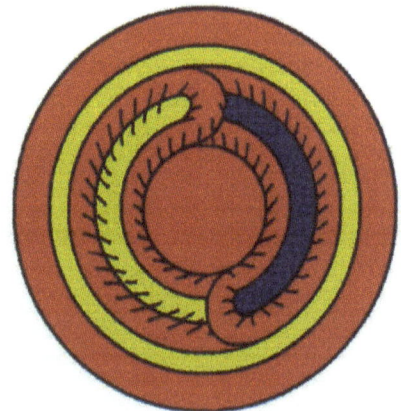

Primani

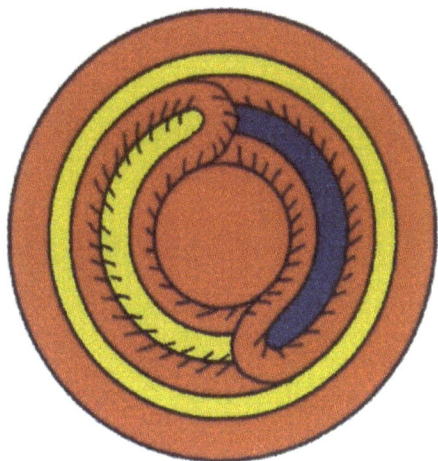

Undecimani

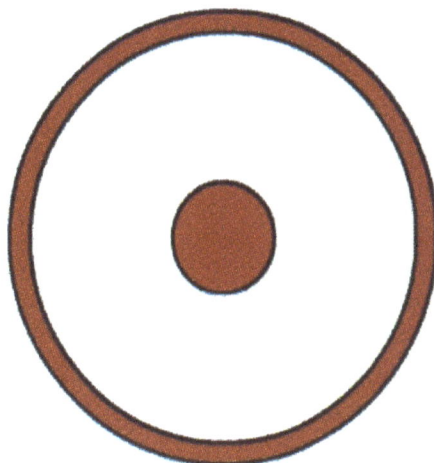

Lanciarii iuniores

Auxilia Palatina

Regii

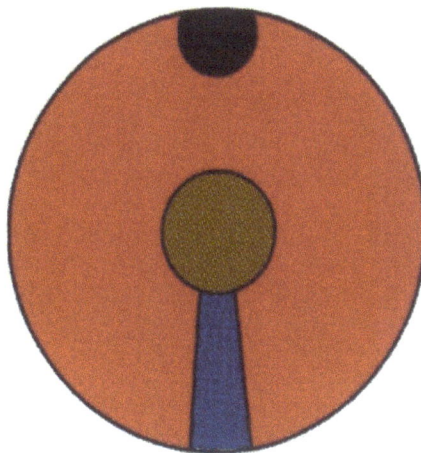

Tubantes

Cornuti

Constantiniani

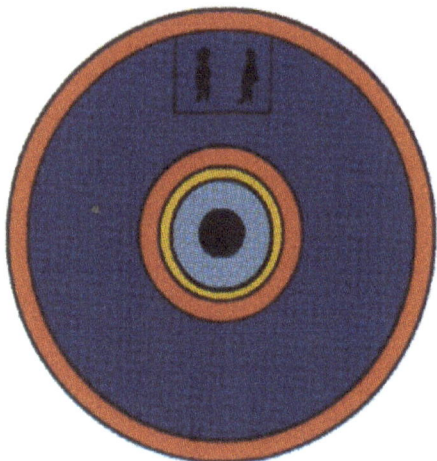

Mattiaci iuniores

Sagittarii dominici

Sagittarii seniores Orientales

Vindices

Sagittarii iuniores Orientales

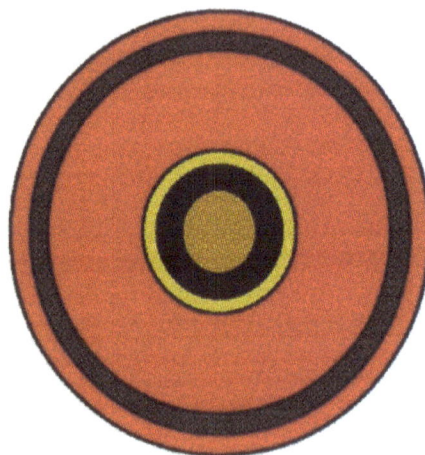

Bucinobantes

GABRIELE ESPOSITO

Falchovarii

Felices Theodosiani

Thraces

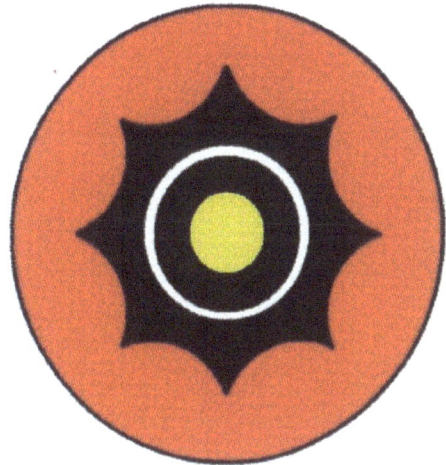

Felices Arcadiani iuniores

Tervingi

Secundi Theodosiani

95

Vexillationes Comitatenses

Equites catafractarii
Equites catafractarii Ambianenses
Equites sexto Dalmatae
Equites secundi scutarii
Equites scutarii
Equites secundi clibanarii Parthi

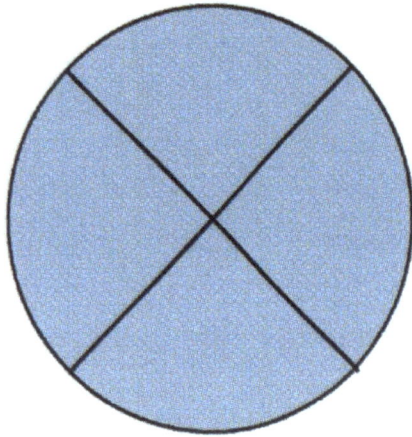

Pseudocomitatenses

Quarti Theodosiani

Vexillationes Palatinae

Equites brachiati iuniores
Equites Batavi iuniores
Equites Persae clibanarii
Equites Theodosiaci seniores
Comites seniores
Comites sagittarii Armeni

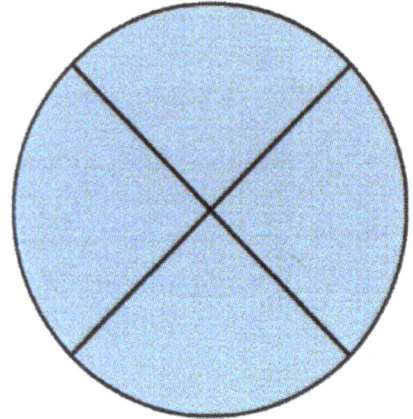

Auxiliarii sagittarii

Magister Militum per Orientem
(commander in the East)

Auxilia Palatina

Felices Arcadiani seniores

Felices Honoriani seniores

Legiones Comitatenses

V Macedonica

X Gemina

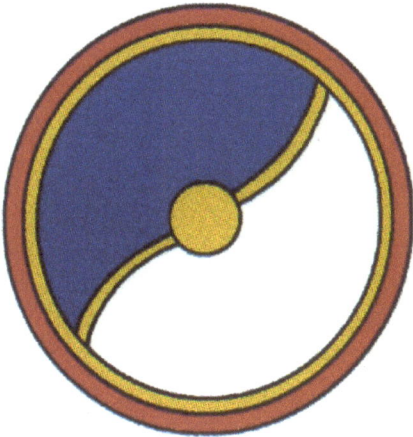

Martenses seniores

Balistarii seniores

VII Gemina

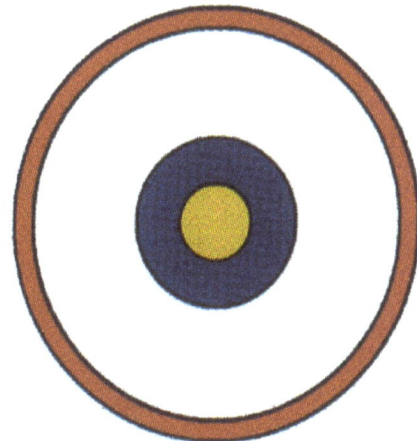

I Flavia Constantia

Vexillationes Comitatenses

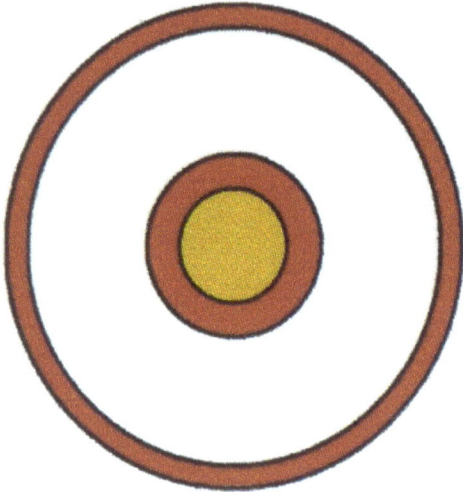

Cuneus equitum secundorum clibanariorum Palmirenorum
Equites armigeri seniores orientales
Equites tertio Dalmatae
Equites primi scutarii Orientales
Equites secundi stablesiani
Equites tertii stablesiani
Equites promoti clibanarii
Equites quarti clibanarii Parthi
Equites primi sagittarii
Comites catafractarii Bucellarii iuniores

Pseudocomitatenses

II Flavia Constantia Thebaeorum

II Felix Valentis Thebaeorum

I Armeniaca

I Flavia Theodosiana

II Armeniaca

Fortenses auxiliarii

IV Italica

Funditores

VI Parthica

I Italica

I Isaura sagittaria

Balistarii Theodosiaci

Transtigritani

Dux Syriae

Legio IV Scythica
Legio XVI Flavia Firma
Cohors I Gotthorum
Cohors I Ulpia Dacorum
Cohors III Valeria
Cohors I victorum
Ala I nova Herculia
Ala I Iuthungorum

Equites scutarii Illyriciani
Equites promoti Illyriciani
Equites sagittarii indigenae (at Matthana)
Equites sagittarii indigenae (at Anatha)
Equites promoti indigenae (at Adada)
Equites promoti indigenae (at Rosafa)
Equites sagittarii (at Acadama)
Equites sagittarii (at Acavatha)
Equites Dalmatae Illyriciani
Equites Mauri Illyriciani

Dux Mesopotamiae

Legio I Parthica Nisibena
Legio II Parthica
Cohors L Arabum
Cohors XIV Valeria Zabdenorum
Ala II nova Aegyptiorum
Ala VIII Flavia Francorum
Ala XV Flavia Carduenorum

Equites scutarii Illyriciani
Equites promoti Illyriciani
Equites ducatores Illyriciani
Equites felices Honoriani Illyriciani
Equites sagittarii indigenae Arabanenses
Equites scutarii indigenae Pafenses
Equites sagittarii indigenae Thibithenses
Equites sagittarii indigenae
Equites promoti indigenae (at Apadna)
Equites promoti indigenae (at Constantina)

Dux Foenicis

Legio I Illyricorum
Legio III Gallica
Cohors III Herculia
Cohors V pacta Alamannorum
Cohors I Iulia lectorum
Cohors II Aegyptiorum
Cohors I Orientalis
Ala I Damascena
Ala nova Diocletiana
Ala I Francorum
Ala I Alamannorum
Ala I Saxonum
Ala I Foenicum
Ala II Salutis

Equites Mauri Illyriciani
Equites scutarii Illyriciani
Equites promoti indigenae (at Saltaha)
Equites promoti indigenae (at Avatha)
Equites promoti indigenae (at Nazala)
Equites sagittarii indigenae (at Abina)
Equites sagittarii indigenae (at Casama)
Equites sagittarii indigenae (at Calamona)
Equites sagittarii indigenae (at Adatha)
Equites Dalmati Illyriciani
Equites Saraceni indigenae
Equites Saraceni

Dux Palaestinae

Legio X Fretensis
Cohors XII Valeria
Cohors X Carthaginensis
Cohors I agentenaria
Cohors IV Frygium
Cohors II Gratiana
Cohors I equitata
Cohors II Galatarum
Cohors I Flavia
Cohors IV Palaestinorum
Cohors II Cretensis
Cohors I salutaria
Ala I miliaria Sebastena
Ala Antana dromedariorum
Ala Constantiana

Ala II felix Valentiana
Ala I miliara
Ala Idiota constituta
Equites Dalmatae Illyriciani
Equites promoti Illyriciani
Equites scutarii Illyriciani
Equites Mauri Illyriciani
Equites Thamudeni Illyriciani
Equites promoti indigenae (at Sabiaea)
Equites promoti indigenae (at Zodocathae)
Equites sagittarii indigenae (at Hauanae)
Equites sagittarii indigenae (at Zoarae)
Equites sagittarii indigenae (at Moahile)
Equites sagittarii indigenae (at Robatha)
Equites primi felices Palaestini

Dux Arabiae

Legio III Cyrenaica
Legio IV Martia
Cohors I miliaria Thracum
Cohors I Thracorum
Cohors VIII voluntaria
Cohors III felix Arabum
Cohors III Alpinorum
Ala IX miliaria
Ala VI Hispanorum
Ala II Constantiana
Ala II Miliarensis

Ala I Valentiana
Ala II felix Valentiniana
Equites scutarii Illyriciani
Equites promoti Illyriciani
Equites Dalmati Illyriciani
Equites Mauri Illyriciani
Equites promoti indigenae (at Speluncis)
Equites promoti indigenae (at Mefa)
Equites sagittari indigenae (at Gadda)
Equites sagittari indigenae (at Diafenis)

Dux Osrhoenae

Legio IV Parthica

Cohors I Gaetulorum

Cohors I Eufratensis

Ala VII Valeria praelectorum

Ala I Victoriae

Ala II Paflagonum

Ala I Parthorum

Ala I nova Diocletiana

Ala I salutaria

Equites Dalmatae Illyriciani

Equites promoti Illyriciani

Equites Mauri Illyriciani

Equites promoti indigenae (at Banasam)

Equites promoti indigenae (at Sina Iudaeorum)

Equites sagittarii indigenae (at Oraba)

Equites sagittarii indigenae (at Thillazamana)

Equites sagittarii indigenae Medianenses

Equites sagittarii indigenae primi Osrhoeni

Dux Armeniae

Legio XV Apollinaris

Legio XII Fulminata

Legio I Pontica

Cohors III Ulpia miliaria Petraeorum

Cohors IV Raetorum

Cohors militaria Bosporiana

Cohors miliaria Germanorum

Cohors I Theodosiana

Cohors Apuleia civium Romanorum

Cohors I Lepidiana

Cohors I Claudia equitata

Cohors II Valentiana

Cohors Mochora

Ala Rizena

Ala Theodosiana

Ala felix Theodosiana

Ala I Augusta Colonorum

Ala Auriana

Ala I Ulpia Dacorum

Ala II Gallorum

Ala castello Tablariensi

Ala I pretorica

Ala I Iovia felix

Ala I felix Theodosiana

Equites sagittarii (at Sabbu)

Equites sagittarii (at Domana)

Comes Limitis Aegypti
(commander of the Egyptian Frontier)

Legio V Macedonica

Legio XIII Gemina

Legio III Diocletiana Thebaidos

Legio II Traiana

Cohors III Galatarum

Cohors II Astarum

Cohors I sagittariorum

Cohors I Augusta Pannoniorum

Cohors I Epireorum

Cohors IV Iuthungorum

Cohors II Ituraeorum

Cohors II Thracum

Cohors IV Numidarum

Ala Theodosiana nuper constituta

Ala Arcadiana nuper constituta

Ala II Armeniorum

Ala III Arabum

Ala VIII Vandilorum

Ala VII Sarmatarum

Ala I Aegyptiorum

Ala veterana Gallorum

Ala I Herculia

Ala V Raetorum

Ala I Tingitana

Ala Apriana

Ala II Assyriorum

Ala V Praelectorum

Ala II Ulpia Afrorum

Ala II Aegyptiorum

Equites stablesiani

Equites Saraceni Thamudeni

GABRIELE ESPOSITO

Dux Thebaidos

Legio III Diocletiana
Legio II Flavia Constantia Thebaeorum
Legio II Traiana
Legio I Valentiniana
Legio I Maximiana
Legio II Valentiniana
Cohors I Lusitanorum
Cohors scutata civium Romanorum
Cohors I Apamenorum
Cohors XI Chamavorum
Cohors IX Tzanorum
Cohors IX Alamannorum
Cohors I felix Theodosiana
Cohors V Suentium
Cohors VI saginarum
Cohors VII Francorum
Ala I Abasgorum
Ala II Hispanorum
Ala Germanorum
Ala IV Britonum
Ala I Hiberorum

Ala Neptunia
Ala III dromedariorum
Ala VIII Palmyrenorum
Ala VII Herculia voluntaria
Ala I Francorum
Ala I Iovia catafractariorum
Ala VIII
Ala II Herculia dromedariorum
Ala I Abasgorum
Ala I Quadorum
Ala I Valeria dromedariorum
Cuneus equitum Maurorum scutariorum
Cuneus equitum scutariorum
Equites sagittarii indigenae (at Tentira)
Equites sagittarii indigenae (at Copto)
Equites sagittarii indigenae (at Diospoli)
Equites sagittarii indigenae (at Lato)
Equites sagittarii indigenae (at Maximianopoli)
Equites promoti indigenae
Equites felices Honoriani
Milites Miliarenses

Magister Militum per Thracias
(commander of Thrace)

Vexillationes Palatinae

Equites Theodosiaci iuniores
Comites Arcadiaci
Comites Honoriaci

Legiones Comitatenses

Solenses seniores

Menapii

103

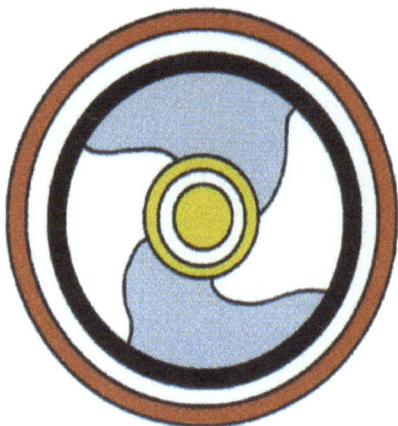

I Maximiana Thebaeorum

Quartodecimani

III Diocletiana Thebaeorum

I Flavia gemina

Tertiodecimani

II Flavia gemina

Constantini seniores

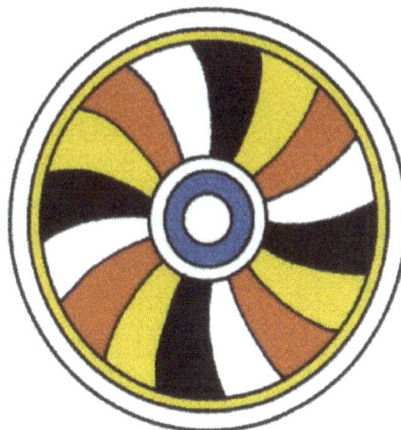

Constantini Dafnenses

Divitenses Gallicani

Balistarii Dafnenses

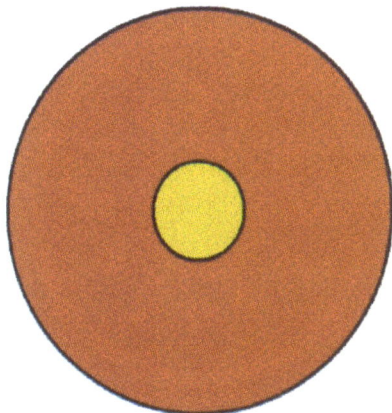

Lanciarii Stobenses

Balistarii iuniores

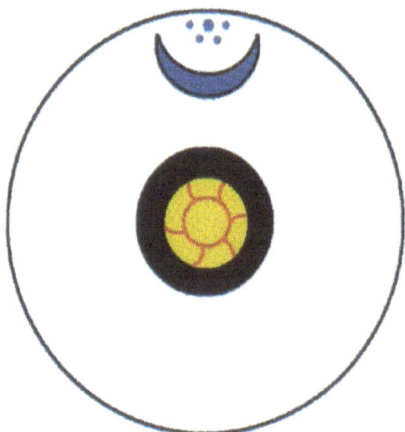

Pannoniciani iuniores

Iulia Alexandria

Tzanni

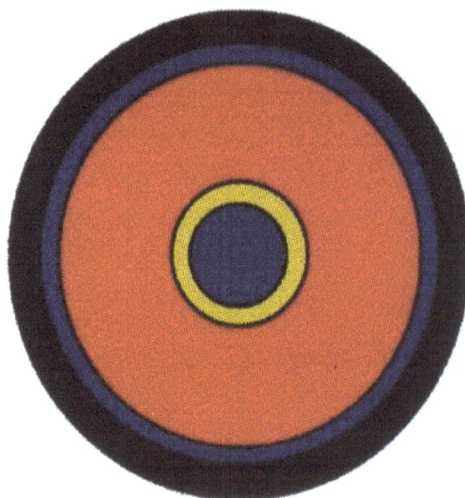

Augustenses

Solenses Gallicani

Valentinianenses

Vexillationes Comitatenses

Equites catafractarii Albigenses
Equites sagittarii seniores
Equites sagittarii iuniores
Equites primi Theodosiani

Gratianenses

Dux Moesiae II

Legio I Italica
Legio XI Claudia
Cohors IV Gallorum
Cohors I Aureliana
Cohors III Valeria Bacarum
Cuneus equitum scutariorum (at Securisca)
Cuneus equitum scutariorum (at Latius)
Cuneus equitum scutariorum (at Appiara)
Cuneus equitum Solensium
Cuneus equitum armigerorum
Cuneus equitum secundorum armigerorum
Cuneus equitum stablesianorum

Milites praeventores
Milites Constantini
Milites Dacisci
Milites tertii navclarii
Milites Novenses
Milites primi Moesiaci
Milites Moesiaci
Milites quarti Constantiani
Milites Cimbriani
Milites navclarii Altinenses
Praefectus navium amnicarum et militum ibidem deputatorum

Dux Scythiae

Legio II Herculia
Legio I Iovia
Cuneus equitum scutariorum
Cuneus equitum Solensium
Cuneus equitum stablesianorum (at Cii)
Cuneus equitum stablesianorum (at Bireo)
Cuneus equitum catafractariorum
Cuneus equitum armigerorum

Cuneus equitum Arcadum
Milites navclarii
Milites superventores
Milites Scythici (at Carso)
Milites Scythici (at Dirigothia)
Milites secundi Constantini
Milites primi Constantini
Milites quinti Constantini
Milites primi Gratianenses

Magister Militum per Illyricum
(commander of Troops in Illyricum)

Legiones Palatinae

Britones seniores

Auxilia Palatina

Ascarii seniores

Ascarii iuniores

Petulantes iuniores

Sagittarii lecti

108

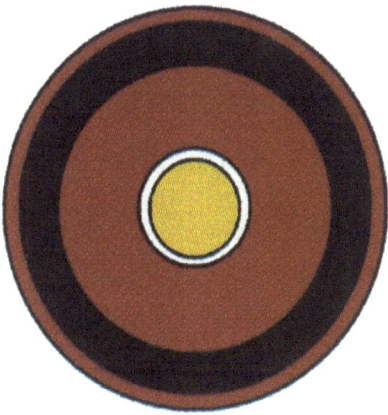

Invicti iuniores

Atecotti

Legiones Comitatenses

Matiarii constantes

Martii

Dianenses

Germaniciani seniores

Secundani

Lanciarii Augustenses

Minervii

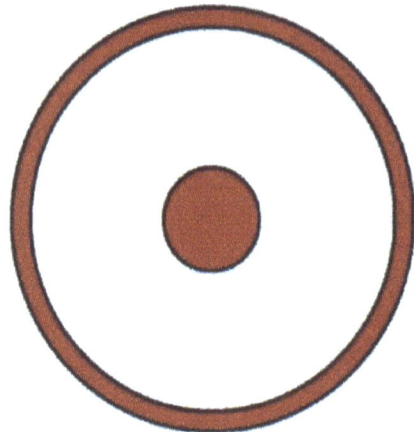

Lanciarii iuniores

Vexillationes Comitatenses

Equites sagittarii seniores

Equites Germaniciani seniores

Pseudocomitatenses

Timacenses auxiliarii
Bugaracenses
Ulpianenses
Secundi Theodosiani
Scampenses

Felices Theodosiani iuniores
Scupenses
Merenses
Balistarii Theodosiani iuniores

Dux Moesiae I

Legio IV Flavia
Legio VII Claudia
Milites exploratores (at Novis)
Milites exploratores (at Taliatae)
Milites exploratores (at Zmirnae)
Milites Vincentiensium
Cuneus equitum Constantiacorum
Cuneus equitum promotorum (at Flaviana)
Cuneus equitum promotorum (at Viminacio)
Cuneus equitum sagittariorum (at Tricornio)
Cuneus equitum sagittariorum (at Laedenatae)
Cuneus equitum Dalmatarum (at Aureomonto)
Cuneus equitum Dalmatarum (at Pinco)
Cuneus equitum Dalmatarum (at Cuppis)
Auxiliares Reginenses
Auxiliares Tricornienses
Auxiliares Novenses
Auxilium Margense
Auxilium Cuppense
Auxilium Gratianense
Auxilium Taliatense
Auxilium Aureomontanum
Classis Histricae
Classis Stradensis et Germensis

Dux Daciae Ripensis

Legio V Macedonica
Legio XIII Gemina
Cohors secundorum reducum
Cohors nova sostica
Milites exploratores
Cuneus equitum Dalmatarum Fortensium
Cuneus equitum Dalmatarum Divitensium (at Dortico)
Cuneus equitum Dalmatarum Divitensium (at Drobeta)
Cuneus equitum scutariorum (at Cebro)
Cuneus equitum scutariorum (at Aegetae)
Cuneus equitum Dalmatarum (at Augustae)
Cuneus equitum Dalmatarum (at Varina)
Cuneus equitum stablesianorum
Cuneus equitum Constantinianorum
Auxilium Miliarentium
Auxilium primorum Daciscorum
Auxilium Crispitienses
Auxilium Mariensium
Auxilium Claustrinorum
Auxilium secundorum Daciscorum
Classis Histricae
Classis Ratianensis

Western Roman army, 410 AD

Magister Officiorum
(commander of the Scholae Palatinae)

Schola scutariorum prima

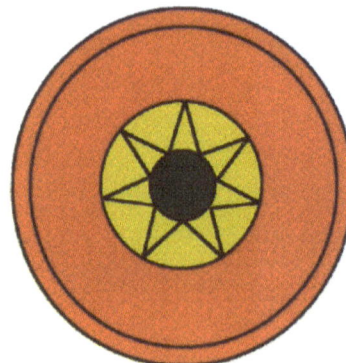

Schola armaturarum seniorum

Schola scutariorum secunda

Schola gentilium seniorum

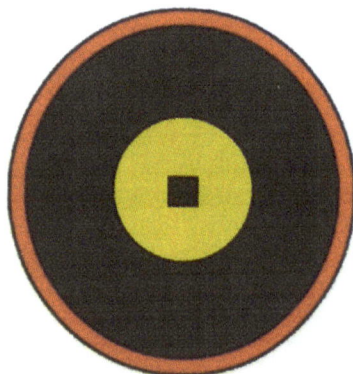

Schola scutariorum tertia

Comes Domesticorum Equitum et Comes Domesticorum Peditum
(commanders of the Protectores)

Domestici equites

Domestici pedites

Magister Peditum Praesentalis
(commander of the Comes Italiae)

Legiones Palatinae

Ioviani seniores

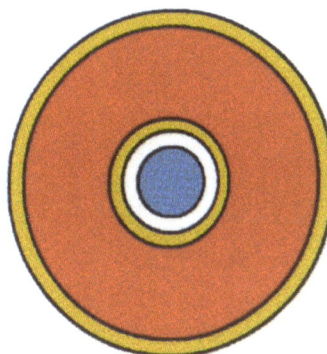

Divitenses seniores

Herculiani seniores

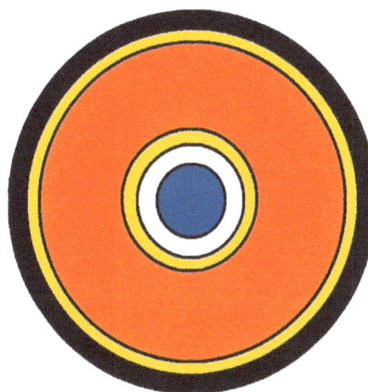

Tongrecani seniores

Pannoniciani seniores

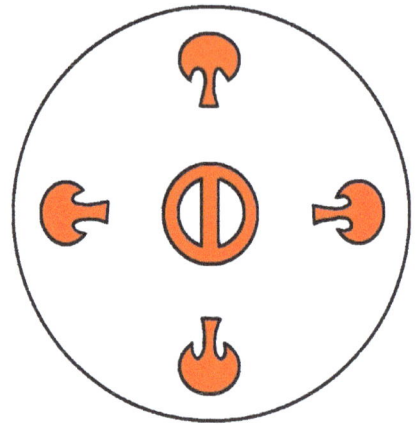

Octavani

Moesiaci seniores

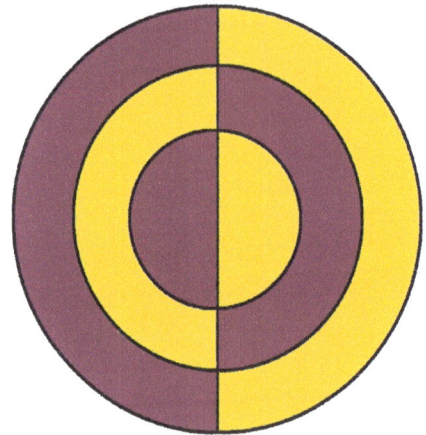

Thebei

Auxilia palatina

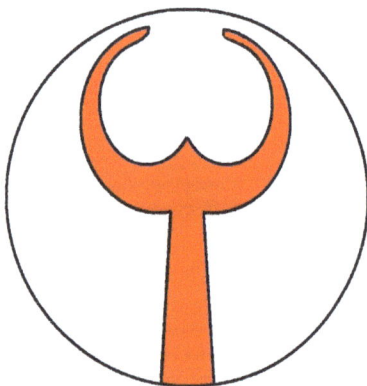

Cornuti seniores

Brachiati seniores

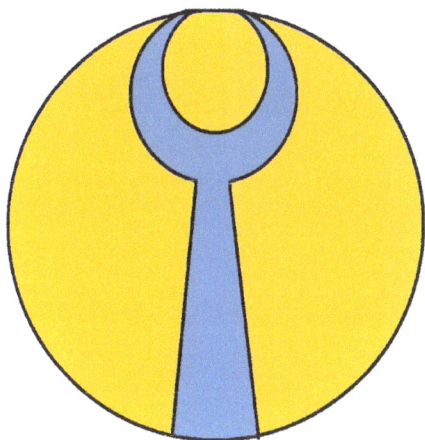

Petulantes seniores

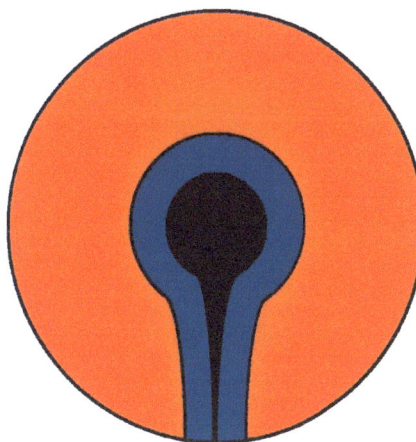

Batavi seniores

Celtae seniores

Mattiaci seniores

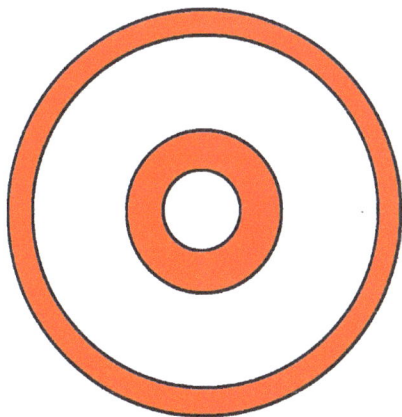

Heruli seniores

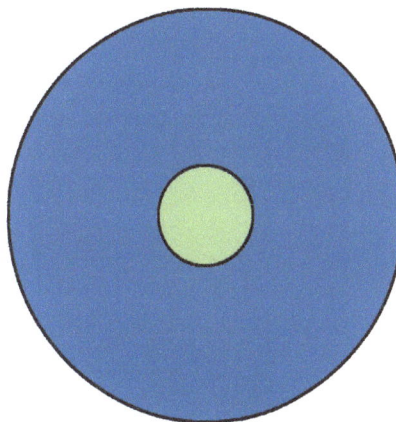

Iovii seniores

Victores seniores

Exculcatores seniores

Cornuti iuniores

Grati

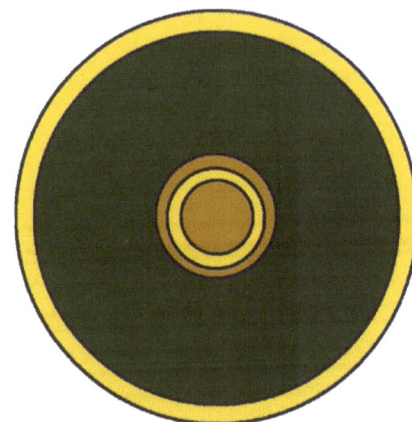

Leones iuniores

Sabini

Felices iuniores

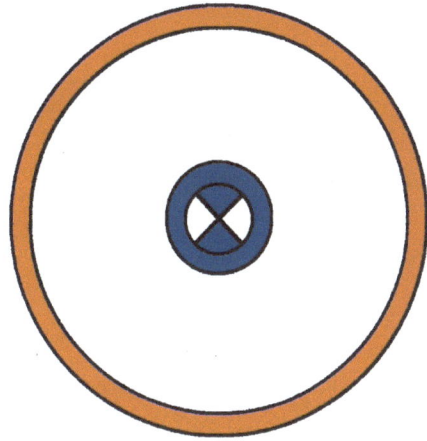

Honoriani Mauri iuniores

Honoriani Atecotti iuniores

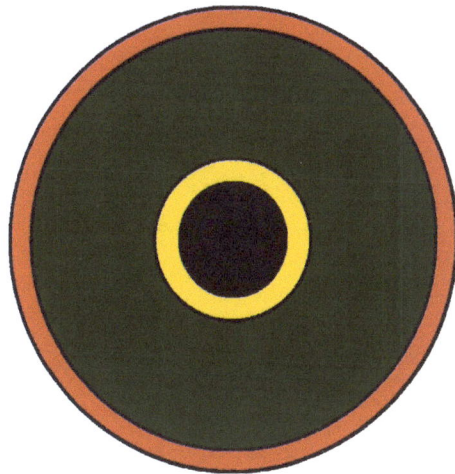

Galli victores

Brisigavi iuniores

Legiones Comitatenses

Mattiarii iuniores

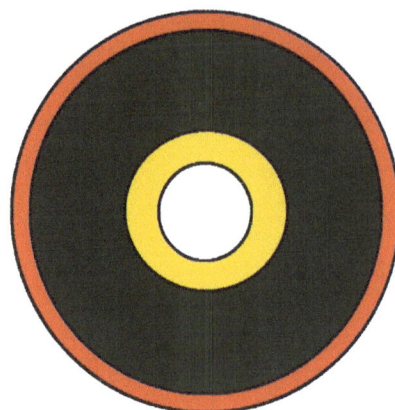

Germaniciani iuniores

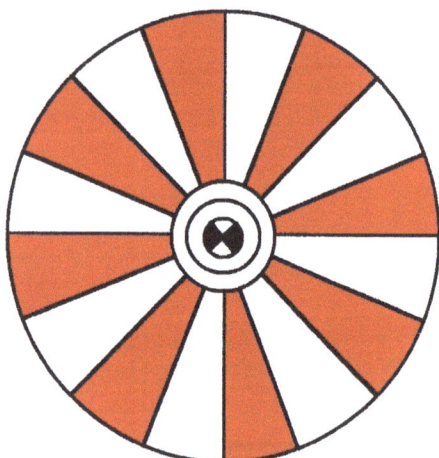

Septimani iuniores

Placidi Valentinianici felices

Regii

Vexillationes Palatinae

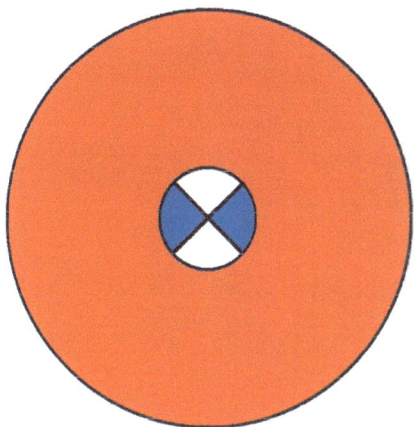

Equites promoti seniores

Equites constantes Valentinianenses iuniores

Equites brachiati seniores

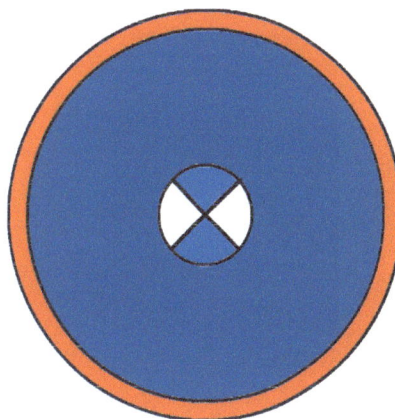

Comites seniores

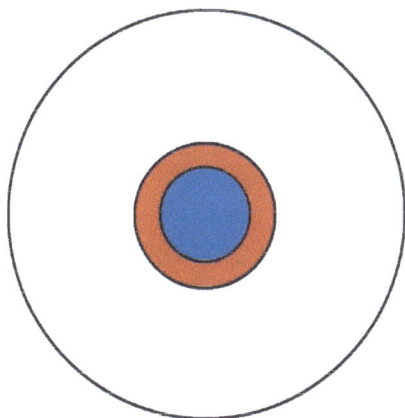

Equites Cornuti seniores

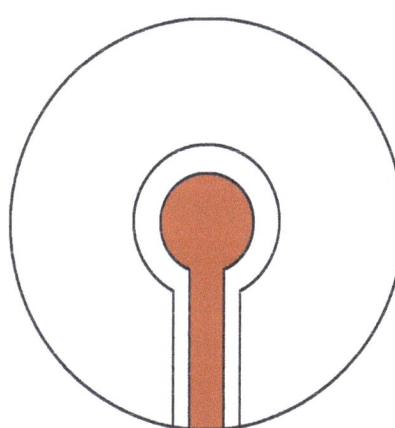

Comites Alani

Vexillationes Comitatenses

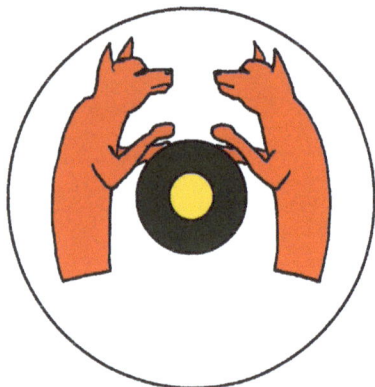

Equites Mauri feroces

Pontinenses

Pseudocomitatenses

I Alpina

Gratianenses iuniores

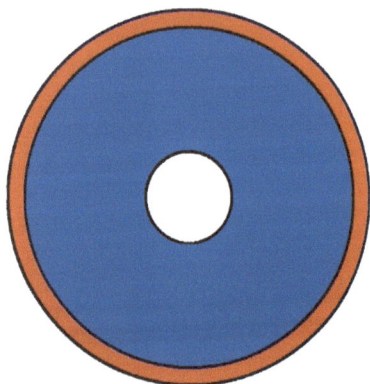

III Iulia Alpina

Marcomanni

Limitanei

Milites iuniores Italici
Sarmati gentiles Apuliae et Calabriae
Sarmati gentiles per Brittios et Lucaniam
Sarmati gentiles (at Foro Fulviensi)
Sarmati gentiles (at Opittergii)
Sarmati gentiles (at Patavio)
Sarmati gentiles (at Cremonae)
Sarmati gentiles (at Taurinis)
Sarmati gentiles (at Novariae)
Sarmati gentiles (at Aquis)

Sarmati gentiles (at Vercellis)
Sarmati gentiles (in Regionis Samnitis)
Sarmati gentiles (at Boniniae)
Sarmati gentiles (at Qudratis and Eporizio)
Sarmati gentiles (at Liguria Pollentia)
Sarmati gentiles (location missing)
Classis Venetum
Classis Ravennatium
Classis Comensis
Classis Misenatium

Magister Equitum Praesentalis
(commander of the Comes Galliae)

Legiones Palatinae

Auxilia Palatina

Lanciarii Sabarienses

Mattiaci iuniores

Leones seniores

Gratianenses seniores

Brachiati iuniores

Bructeri

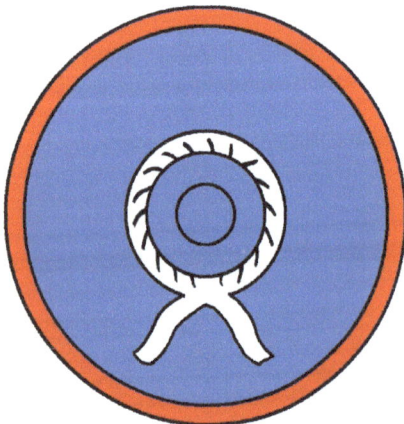

Salii seniores

Ampsivarii

Valentianenses iuniores

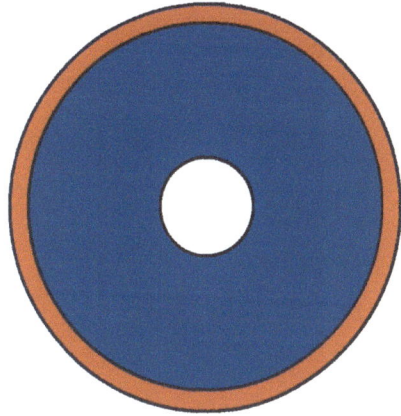

Honoriani Atecotti seniores

Batavi iuniores

Sagittarii Nervi Gallicani

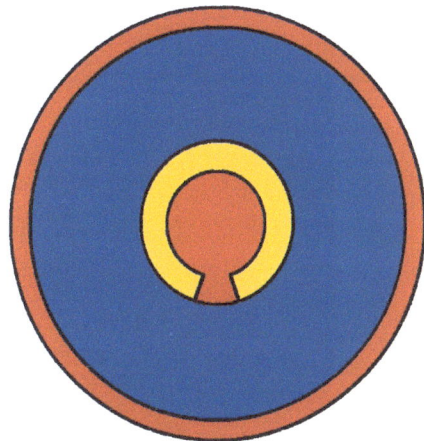

Britones

Iovii iuniores Gallicani

Legiones Comitatenses

Mattiaci iuniores Gallicani

Armigeri defensores seniores

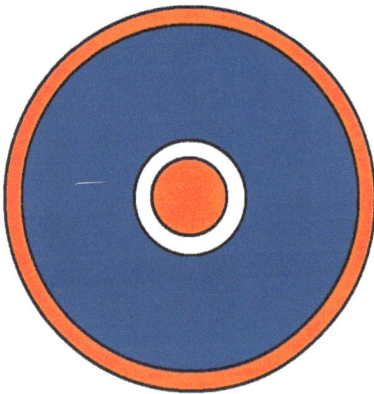

Atecotti iuniores Gallicani

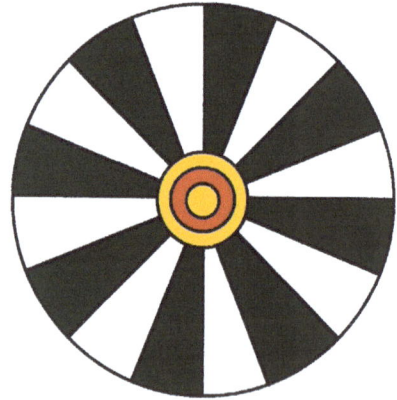

Lanciarii Gallicani Honoriani

Honoriani ascarii seniores

Menapi seniores

II Britannica

Geminiacenses

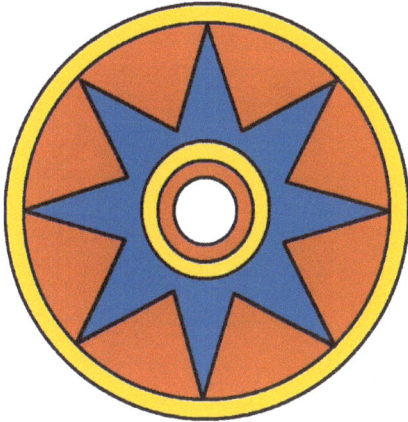

Ursarienses

Cortoriacenses

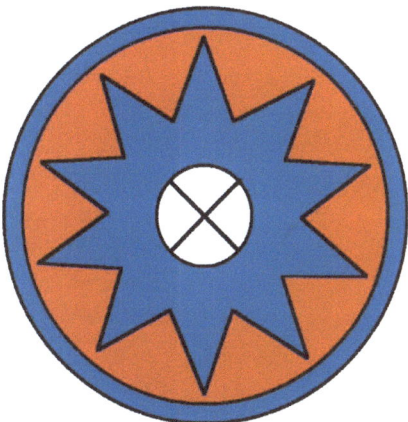

Praesichantes

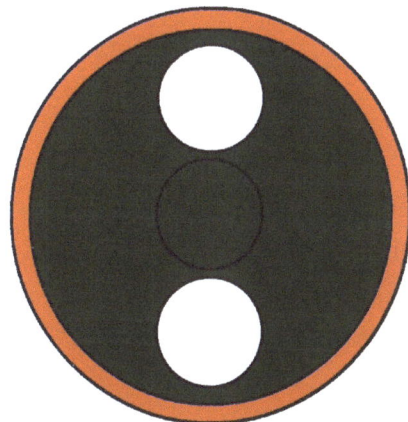

Honoriani felices Gallicani

Vexillationes Palatinae

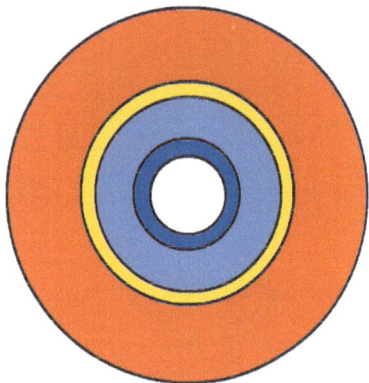

Equites Batavi seniores

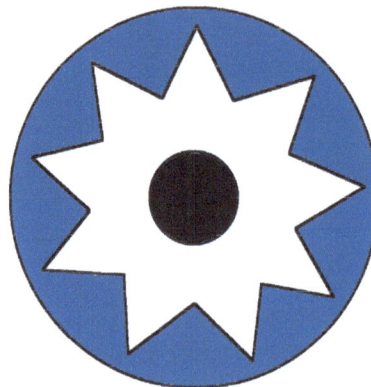

Equites Batavi iuniores

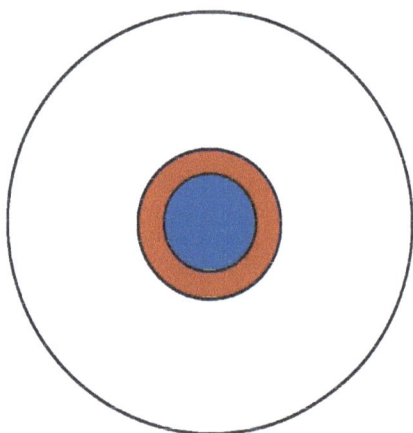

Equites Cornuti seniores

Equites Brachiati iuniores

Vexillationes Comitatenses

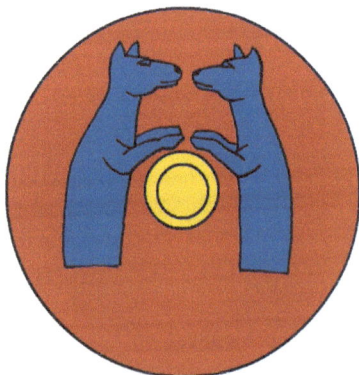

Equites Honoriani seniores

Equites Honoriani iuniores

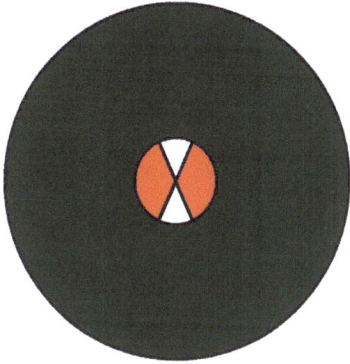

Equites armigeri seniores

Equites primi Gallicani

Equites octavo Dalmatae

Equites Mauri alites

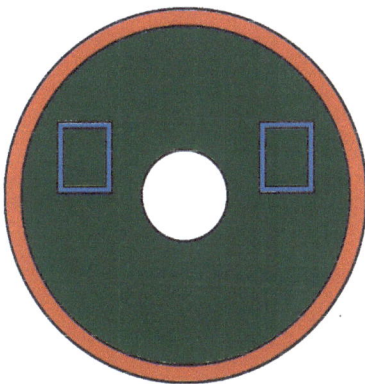

Equites Dalmatae Passerentiacenses

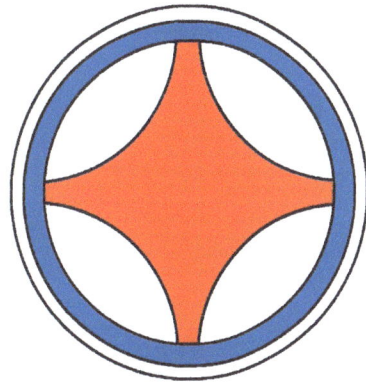

Equites Constantiaci feroces

Pseudocomitatenses

I Flavia Gallicana Constantia

Defensores seniores

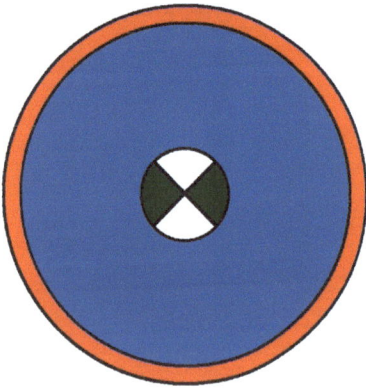

Martenses

Mauri Osismiaci

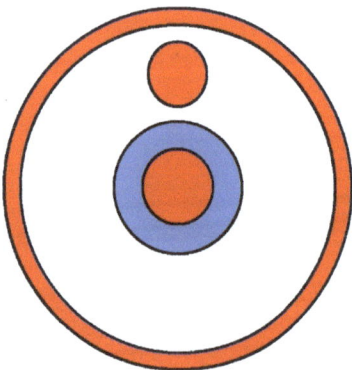

Abrincateni

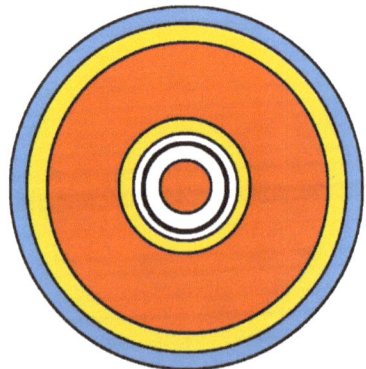

I Flavia Metis

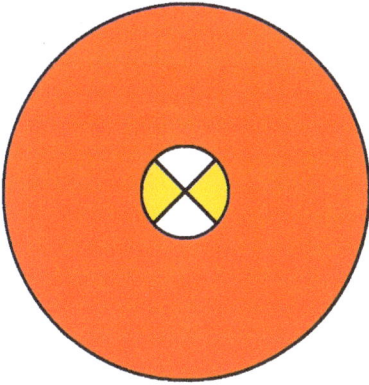

Superventores iuniores
Balistarii
Defensores iuniores
Garronenses
Anderetiani
Acincenses
Corniacenses

Cursarienses iuniores
Musmagenses
Insidatores
Truncensimani
Abulci
Exploratores

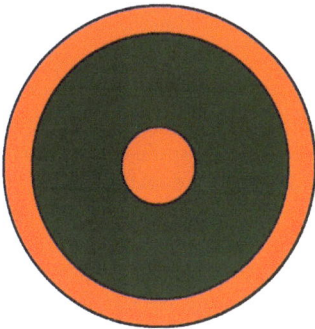

Septimani

Limitanei

Cohors I Flavia Sapaudica
Cohors Noevempopulana
Milites muscularii
Sarmati et Taifali gentiles (in Pictavi)
Sarmati gentiles (in Chora Parisios)
Sarmati gentiles (in Belgica secunda)
Sarmati gentiles (in Rodunensem and Alaunorum)
Sarmati gentiles (at Lingonas)
Sarmati gentiles (location missing)
Laeti gentiles (at Remo and Silvamectum)
Laeti gentiles Suevi (at Ceromannos)
Laeti gentiles Suevi (at Arumbernos)

Romanenses

Laeti Batavi et gentiles Suevi
Laeti Batavi Nemetacenses
Laeti Batavi Contraginnenses
Laeti Teutoniciani
Laeti Franci
Laeti Lingonenses
Laeti Acti
Laeti Nervii
Laeti Lagenses
Classis fluminis Rhodani
Classis barcariorum
Classis Araricae
Classis Anderetianorum

Dux Sequanicae

Milites Latavienses

Dux Tractus Armoricani et Nervicani

Cohors I nova Armoricana
Milites Carronenses
Milites Mauri Benetori
Milites Mauri Osimaci
Milites Superventores

Milites Martenses
Milites I Flavia
Milites Ursarienses
Milites Dalmatii
Milites Grannonenses

Dux Belgicae Secundae

Milites Nervii
Equites Dalmatae
Sarmati gentiles
Laeti gentiles

Laeti Nervii
Laeti Batavi Nemetacenses
Laeti Batavi Contraginnenses
Classis Sambricae

Dux Mogontiacensis

Milites Pacenses
Milites Menapi
Milites Anderetiani
Milites Vindici
Milites Martenses
Milites II Flavia

Milites armigeri
Milites Bingenses
Milites balistarii
Milites defensores
Milites Acincenses

Comes Britanniae
(commander of Britain)

Auxilia Palatina

Victores iuniores Britanniciani

Legiones Comitatenses

Primani iuniores
Secundani iuniores

Vexillationes Comitatenses

Equites catafractarii iuniores   *Equites stablesiani*
Equites scutarii Aureliaci   *Equites Syri*

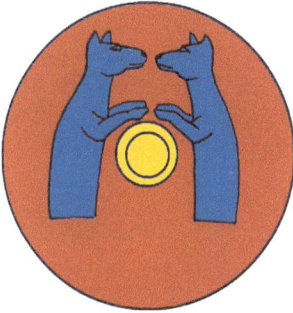

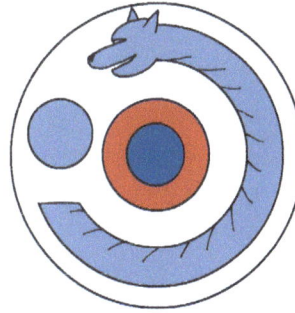

Equites Honoriani seniores   *Equites Honoriani Taifali iuniores*

Dux Britanniarum

Legio VI Victrix   *Cohors II Dalmatarum*
Numerus Barcarii Tigrisienses   *Cohors I Aelia Dacorum*
Numerus Nervii Dictenses   *Cohors II Lingonum*
Numerus Vigilium   *Cohors I Hispanorum*
Numerus Exploratores   *Cohors II Thracum*
Numerus Directorum   *Cohors I Aelia Classica*
Numerus Defensorum   *Cohors I Morinorum*
Numerus Solenses   *Cohors III Nerviorum*
Numerus Pacenses   *Cohors VI Nerviorum*
Numerus Longovicaniorum   *Ala I Asturum*
Numerus Supervenientium Petueriensium   *Ala Sabiniana*
Numerus Maurorum Aurelianorum   *Ala II Asturum*
Cohors IV Lingona   *Ala Petriana*
Cohors I Cornovii   *Ala I Herculea*
Cohors I Frixagorum   *Cuneus Sarmatarum*
Cohors I Batavorum   *Equites Dalmatarum*
Cohors I Tungororum   *Equites Crispianorum*
Cohors IV Gallorum   *Equites Catafractariorum*
Cohors I Asturum

Comes Litoris Saxonici per Britannias

Legio II Augusta

Numerus Fortensium

Numerus Turnacensium

Numerus Abulcorum

Numerus Exploratorum

Cohors I Baetasiorum

Milites Tungrecanorum

Equites Dalmatarum Branodunensium

Equites Stablesianorum Gariannonensium

Comes Illyrici
(commander of Troops in Illyricum)

Auxilia Palatina

Sagittarii Tungri

Sequani

Iovii iuniores

Reti

Sagittarii venatores

Honoriani victores

Latini

Seguntienses

Felices Valentinianenses

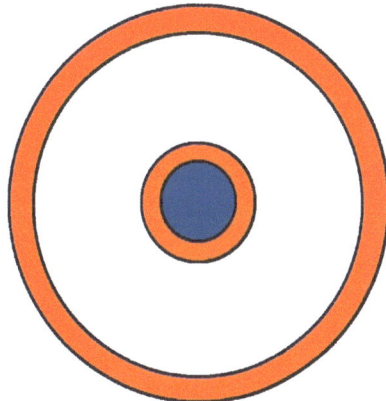

Tungri

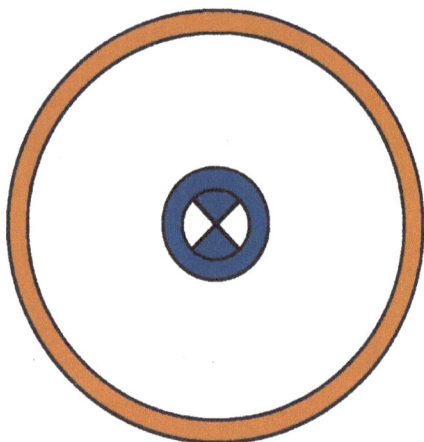

Mauri Honoriani seniores

Catarienses

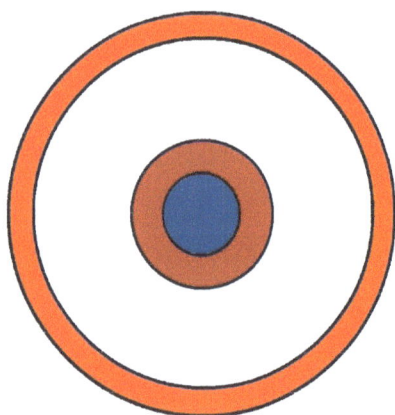

Mattiarii Honoriani Gallicani

Valentinianenses

Legiones comitatenses

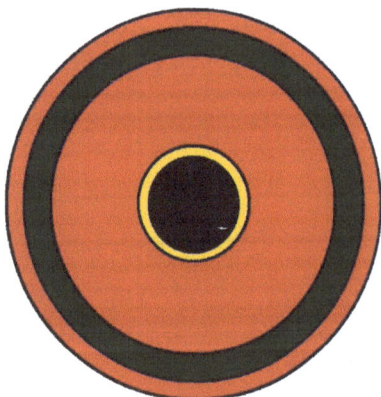

Tertiani

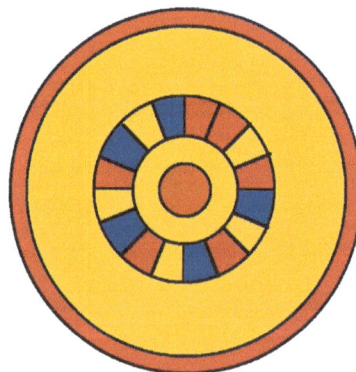

III Herculea

Pseudocomitatenses

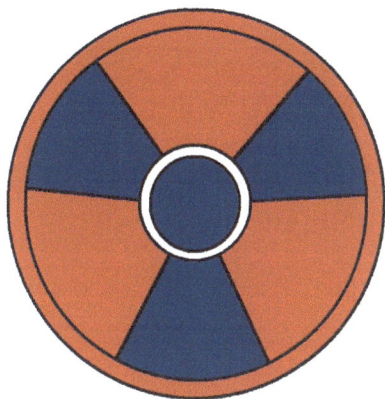

Pacatianenses

Lanciarii Lauriacenses

Mauri cetrati

Lanciarii Comaginenses

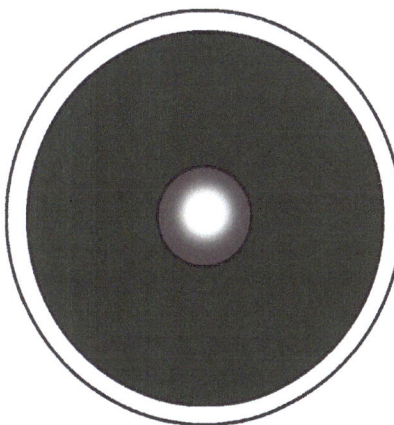

Propugnatores iuniores

II Iulia Alpina

Dux Raetiae I et II

Legio III Italica
Numerus barbaricariorum
Cohors nova Batavorum
Cohors III Brittonum
Cohors VI Valeria Raetorum
Cohors I Herculea Raetorum
Cohors V Valeria Frygum
Cohors III Herculea Pannoniorum
Cohors Herculea Pannoniorum

Milites Ursarienses
Ala I Flavia Raetorum
Ala II Valeria singularis
Ala II Valeria Sequanorum
Equites stablesiani seniores
Equites stablesiani iuniores (at Ponte Aoni)
Equites stablesiani iuniores (at Submuntorio)
Gentes per Raetias deputatae

Dux Pannoniae I et Norici Ripensis

Legio X Gemina
Legio XIV Gemina
Legio II Italica
Legio I Noricorum
Cohors (no name given, at Arrianis)
Cohors (no name given, at Caratensis)
Cohors (no name given, at Boiodoro)
Cohors (no name given, at Austuris)
Cohors (no name given, at Cannabiaca)
Cuneus equitum Dalmatarum
Cuneus equitum stablesianorum
Equites promoti (at Arrabonae)
Equites promoti (at Flexo)
Equites promoti (at Mauros)

Equites promoti (at Comagenis)
Equites sagittarii (at Quadriburgio)
Equites sagittarii (at Gerolate)
Equites sagittarii (at Lentiae)
Equites sagittarii (at Lacufelis)
Equites Dalmatae (at Ala Nova)
Equites Dalmatae (at Aequinoctoiae)
Equites Dalmatae (at Ad Herculem)
Equites Dalmatae (at Arlape)
Equites Dalmatae (at Augustianis)
Equites Mauri
Gentes Marcomannorum
Classis Histricae
Classis Arlapensis et Maginensis
Classis Lauriacensis

Dux Pannoniae II

Legio VI Herculea
Legio V Iovia
Cohors III Alpina Dardanorum
Cohors III Alpina
Cohors I Iovia
Cohors I Thraci Cives Romanorum
Milites Calicarienses
Auxilia Herculensia
Auxilia Novensia
Auxilia Augustensia
Auxilia Praesidentia
Auxilia Ascarii
Ala Sirmienses
Cuneus Equitum Scutariorum
Cuneus Equitum Dalmatarum

Cuneus Equitum Constantianorum
Cuneus Equitum Promotorum
Cuneus Equitum Constantium
Cuneus Equitum Italicianorum
Equites Dalmatae (at Novas)
Equites Dalmatae (at Albano)
Equites Dalmatae (at Cornaco)
Equites Dalmatae (at Ricti)
Equites Dalmatae (at Burgentas)
Equites Dalmatae (at Bornoriae)
Equites Dalmatae (at Cusi)
Equites promoti (at Teutibarcio)
Equites promoti (at Tauruno)
Equites sagittarii (at Cuccis)
Equites sagittarii (at Acimirci)

Classis I Flavia Augusta
Classis II Flavia
Classis Histricae

Classis I Pannonica
Classis II Pannonica

Dux Valeriae Ripensis

Legio I Adiutrix
Legio II Adiutrix
Cohors (no name given, at Vincentiae)
Cohors (no name given, at Quadriborgio)
Cohors (no name given, at Iovia)
Cohors (no name given, at Borgum Centenarium)
Cohors (no name given, at Alescae)
Cohors (no name given, at Marinanae)
Auxilia Herculentia
Auxilia Ursarentia
Auxilia vigilum
Auxilia Fortensia
Auxilia insidiatorum
Cuneus equitum scutatorum
Cuneus equitum Dalmatarum
Cuneus equitum Constantianorum
Cuneus equitum stablesianorum
Cuneus equitum Fortensium

Equites Dalmatae (at Odiabo)
Equites Dalmatae (at Ad Herculem)
Equites Dalmatae (at Cirpi)
Equites Dalmatae (at Constantiae)
Equites Dalmatae (at Campona)
Equites Dalmatae (at Vetusalinae)
Equites Dalmatae (at Adnamantia)
Equites Dalmatae (at Lussonio)
Equites Dalmatae (at Ripa Alta)
Equites Dalmatae (at Ad Statuas)
Equites Dalmatae (at Florentiae)
Equites promoti (at Crumero)
Equites promoti (at Matrice)
Equites sagittarii (at Intercisa)
Equites sagittarii (at Altino)
Equites Mauri
Equites Flavianenses
Classis Histricae

Comes Africae
(commander of Africa)

Legiones Palatinae

Armigeri propugnatores seniores

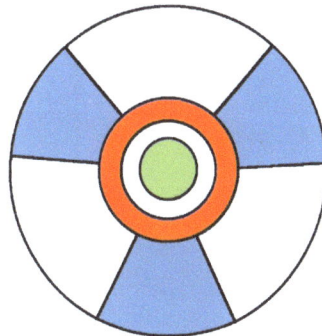

Armigeri propugnatores iuniores

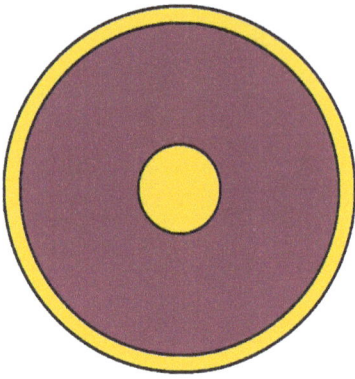

Cimbriani

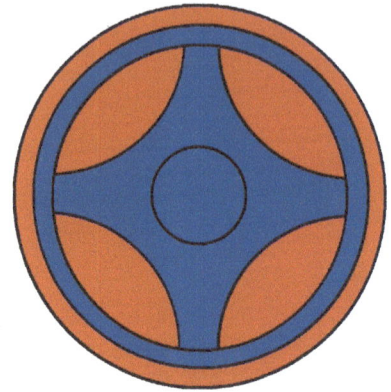

Primani

Auxilia Palatina

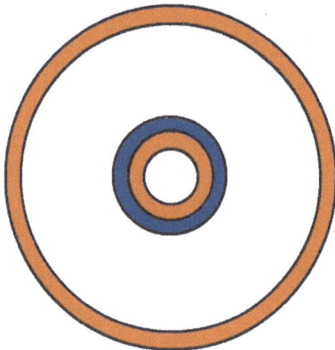

Celtae iuniores

Secundani

Legiones Comitatenses

Secundani Italiciani

Tertiani

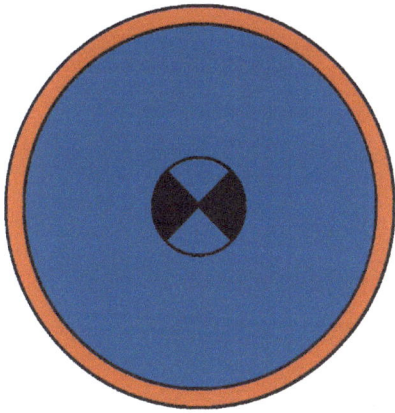

Constantiniani

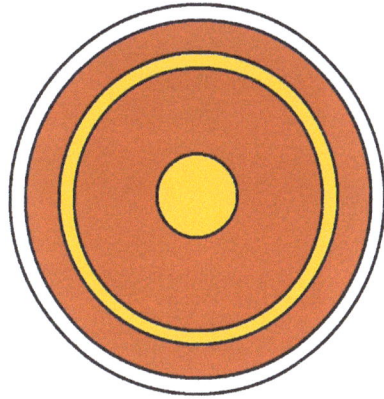

Tertio Augustani

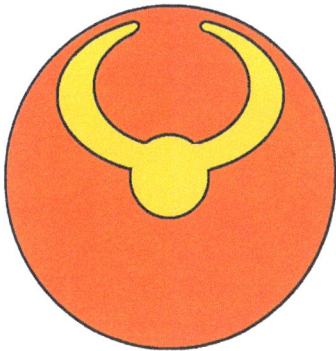

Constantiaci

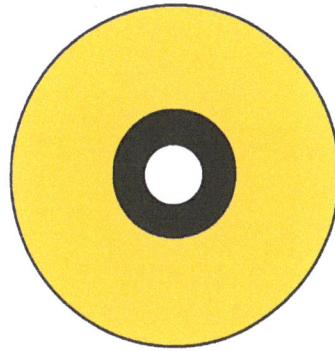

Fortenses

Vexillationes Comitatenses

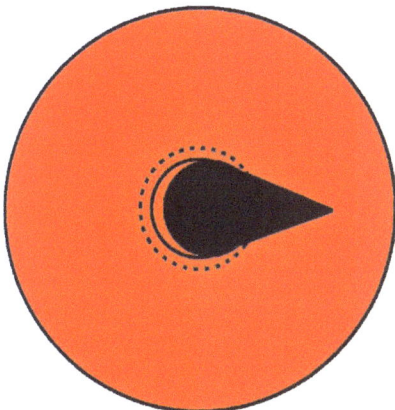

Equites stablesiani italiciani

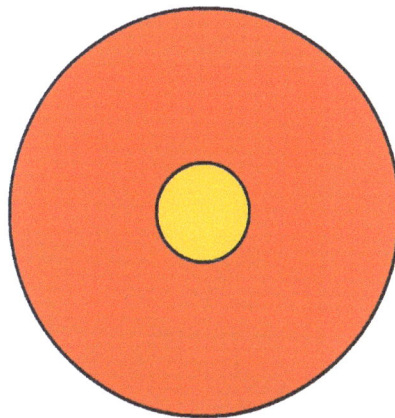

Equites scutarii seniores

Equites stablesiani seniores

Equites clibanarii

Equites Marcomanni

Equites Panthosagittarii seniores

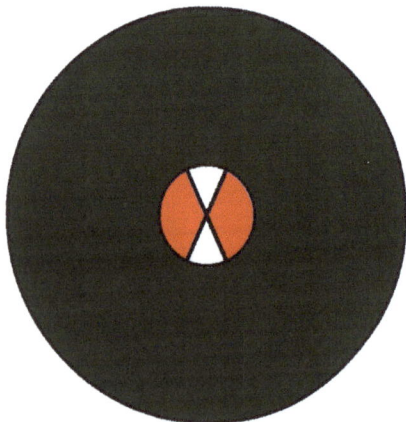

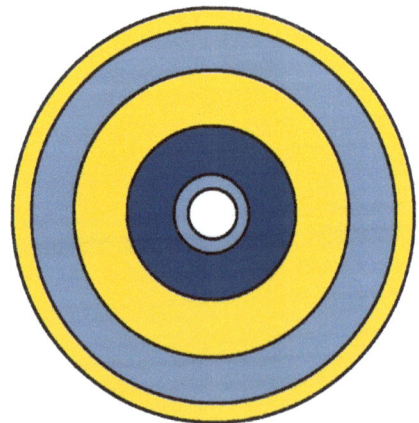

Equites armigeri seniores

Equites cetrati seniores

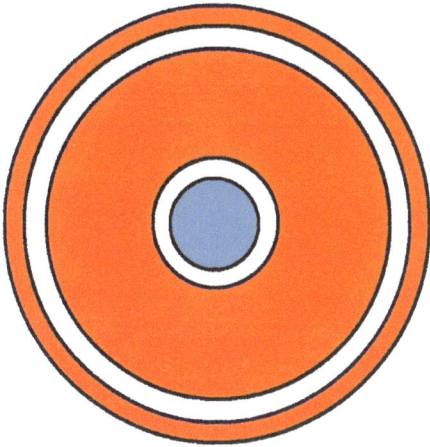

Equites sagittarii primi

Equites quarto sagittarii

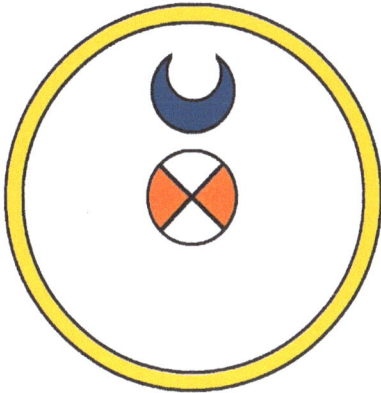

Equites secundo sagittarii

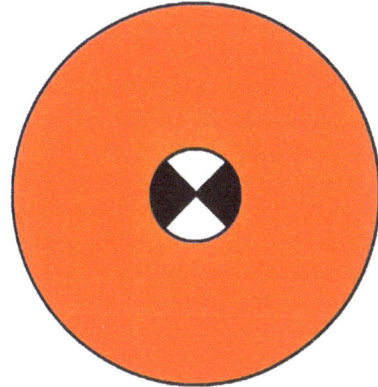

Equites Parthi sagittarii iuniores

Equites tertio sagittarii

Equites crinati iuniores

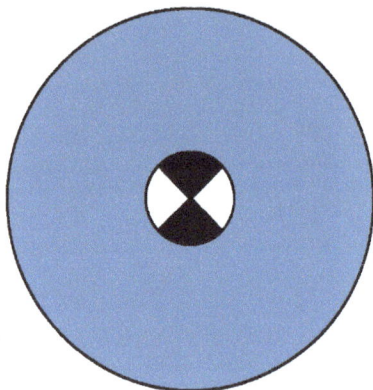

Equites promoti iuniores

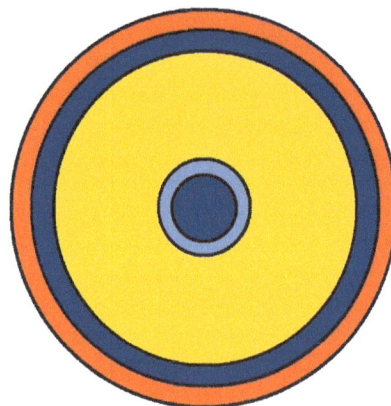

Equites scutarii iuniores scholae secundi

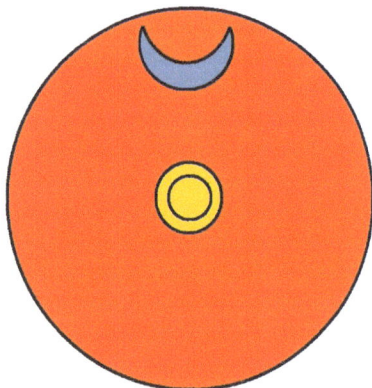

Equites scutarii iuniores comitatenses

Equites armigeri iuniores

Limitanei

Limitanei Thamallensis
Limitanei Montensis
Limitanei Bazensis
Limitanei Gemellensis
Limitanei Tubuniensis
Limitanei Zabensis
Limitanei Tubusubditani
Limitanei Thamallomensis
Limitanei Balaretensis
Limitanei Columnatensis
Limitanei Tablatensis
Limitanei Caputcellensis

Equites Honoriani iuniores

Limitanei Secundaeforum
Limitanei Taugensis

Limitanei Bidensis
Limitanei Badensis

Dux Tripolitaniae

Milites Fortenses in castris Leptitanis
Milites Munifices in castris Madensibus
Limitanei Talalatensis
Limitanei Tenthettani
Limitanei Bizerentane
Limitanei Tillibarensis
Limitanei Madensis

Limitanei Maccomadensis
Limitanei Tintiberitani
Limitanei Bubensis
Limitanei Mamucensis
Limitanei Balensis
Limitanei Varensis
Limitanei Sarcitani

Dux Mauretaniae Caesariensis

Limitanei Columnatensis
Limitanei Vidensis
Limitanei inferioris
Limitanei Fortensis

Limitanei Muticitani
Limitanei Audiensis
Limitanei Caput cellensis
Limitanei Augustensis

Comes Tingitaniae
(commander of Mauretania Tingitania)

Auxilia Palatina

Mauri tonantes seniores

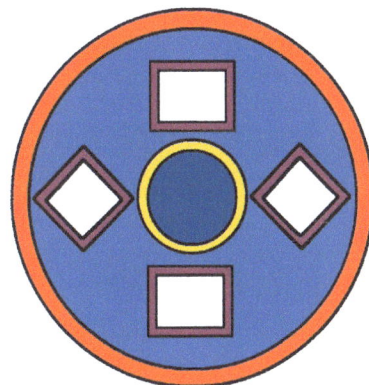

Mauri tonantes iuniores

Legiones Comitatenses

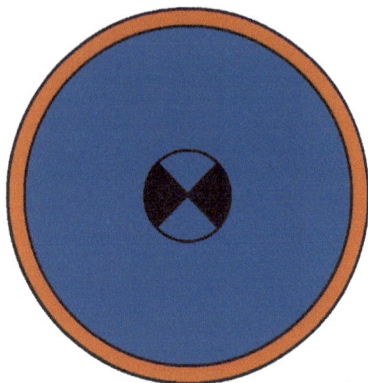

Constantiniani

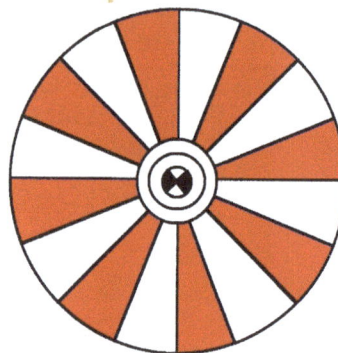

Septimani iuniores

Vexillationes Comitatenses

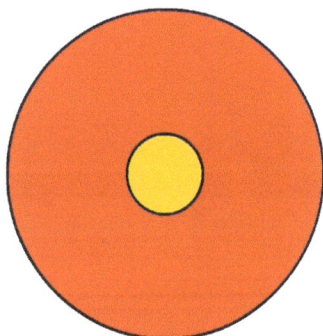

Equites scutarii seniores comitatenses

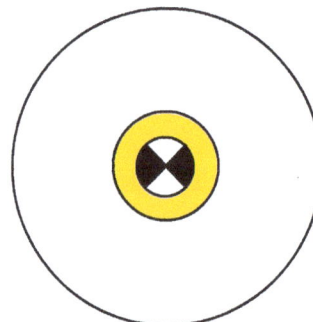

Equites Cardueni comitatenses

Limitanei

Cohors II Hispanorum
Cohors I Herculeae
Cohors I Ityraeorum
Cohors Pacatianensis
Cohors III Hastorum
Cohors Friglensis
Cohors (no name given, at Sala)
Ala Herculea

Equites sagittarii seniores comitatenses

Comes Hispaniae
(commander of Spain)

Auxilia Palatina

Ascarii seniores

Exculcatores iuniores

Ascarii iuniores

Tubantes

Sagittarii nervi

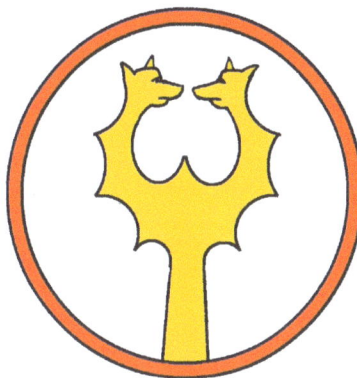

Felices seniores

Invicti seniores

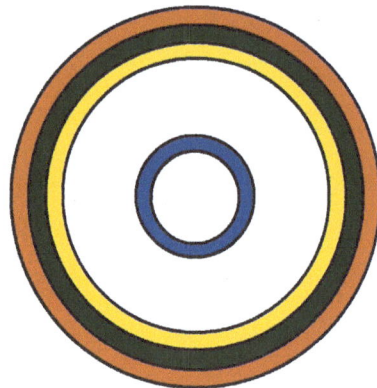

Brisigavi seniores

Victores iuniores

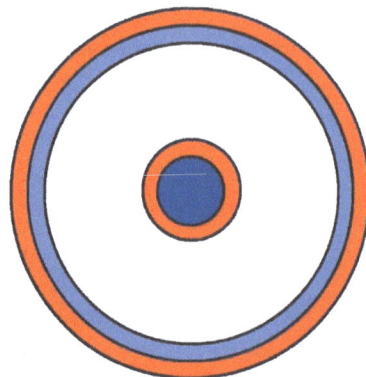

Salii iuniores Gallicani

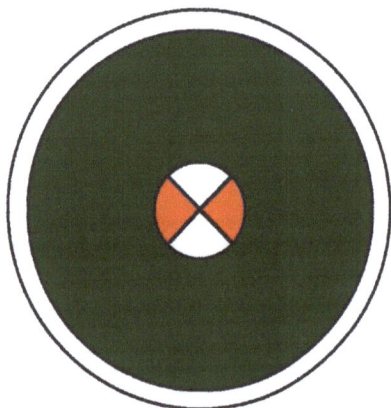

Invicti iuniores Britones

Legiones Comitatenses

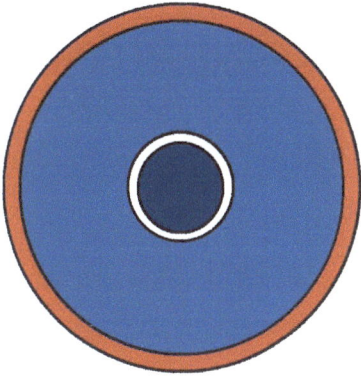

Fortenses

Vesontes

Propugnatores seniores

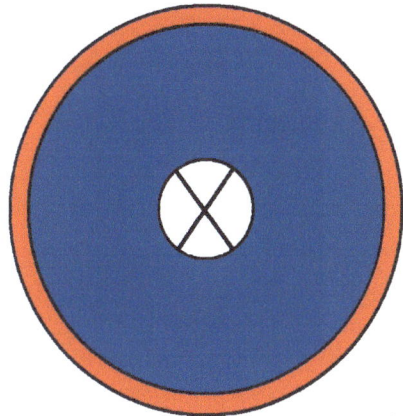

Undecimani

Limitanei

Legio VII Gemina
Cohors II Flavia Pacatiana
Cohors II Gallica
Cohors Lucensis
Cohors Celtiberae
Cohors I Gallica

Septimani seniores

Glossary – Places and Things

Adiutor - new kind of subordinate rank in the late legions, acting as a record keeper of the legio.

Ala – cavalry unit, numbering around 600 soldiers in the late Empire.

Alemanni – a confederation of Germanic tribes on the upper Rhine

Annonae Civicae – extra rations often doled out to the guard units

Arcubus Ligneis – wooden bow

Armaturae - armour

Auxilia or Auxiliaries - the non-citizen troops.

Auxilia palatina - infantry units of the late Roman Army first raised by Constantine I for the new field armies in 325 AD.

Biarchus - officer commanding half century

Bucellarii - a term for the sort of soldiers in the late Roman or Byzantine Empires who were raised by an individual such as a general or governor. In essence they were small private armies equipped and paid by wealthy influential people. As such they were quite often better trained and equipped, not to mention motivated, than the regular soldiers of the time.

Burgarii – defenders of a frontier fort

Campidoctor - drill instructor

Centurion - a professional officer of the Roman army commanding a "century" of about 100 men. Their symbol of office was the vine staff which could be used to discipline soldiers or civilians.

Clavii - decorative stripes of the late Roman tunic

Cataphract - a form of heavily armored cavalry initially developed by the Parthians and Sassanids and later by the Romans. They were usually armed with a long two-handed lance (kontos) useful for charging across large plains. In addition to the men, the horses were also armored.

Cohort - the basic tactical unit of an Imperial Roman legion.

Contubernia - the smallest organized units of soldiers in the Imperial Roman Army, composed of eight legionaries known as a contubernium who shared a tent. They shared punishment and reward as a group.

Ten contubernia were grouped into a century.

Comes excubitorum - the commander of the Excubitores.

Comitatenses – the field units of the late Roman Empire.

Comitatus Praesentalis - the field army under the Emperor's control.

Comites or **Comes** – sometimes translated as "counts", was the leading military commander of the Diocese.

Cuneus – was a cavalry unit numbering 256 men and similar to tarantiarchia, but based on Hun formations.

Dalmatae - were an ancient people who inhabited the core of what would then become known as Dalmatia.

Decanus - the equivalent of a junior NCO, appointed from within the contubernium from the longest serving legionary.

Decurio - an officer in the Roman cavalry, originally commanding a troop of ten men (decuria). During the late empire a decurio commanded a turma of 32 men.

Dediticii - one of the three classes of barbarians living in the Empire. The dediticii were neither slaves, nor Roman citizens.

Domesticus - a member of the protectores domestici, who were an elite guard unit of the Emperor in the late Roman Army.

Draconarius - a type of signifer who carried the draco cavalry standard. The draco was introduced in the fourth century as a Roman standard and consisted of a bronze dragon head with a fabric body similar in shape to a tail attached behind it. Wind flowed through the gaping mouth and billowed out the cloth tail much like a windsock. Some historians have hypothesized that some form of whistle was mounted in the dragon's neck to make a terrifying noise when galloping.

Dura Europos also spelled **Dura Europus** – a border city built on the Euphrates River in the Hellenistic period. It was captured by the Romans in 165 and destroyed during a siege by the Sassanid's in 257. It was abandoned and covered over until being rediscovered in the twentieth century. A great deal of equipment was preserved in place including a painted shield.

Dux - the highest military office within late Roman provinces. Once authorized by the provincial governor, the dux could act independently from him and handled all military matters.

Equites - originally is was the lower of the two patrician orders. By the late empire this term meant "cavalrymen" or "cavalry units".

Equites Singulares Augusti - Mounted bodyguard of the Emperors.

Equites Stablesiani - a class of cavalry created during the reign of Gallienus (260-268) as regimental formations.

Excubitores - a guard unit founded by the Emperor Leo I about 460. They numbered around 300 men recruited from the Isaurians to counter-balance the Germanic element in the Eastern Roman Army.

Foederati – The regular foederati in the west or symmachi in the east were both forces supplied by barbarian chiefs under their treaty of alliance with Rome.

Fortlets - small forts built along intervals of a wall.

Franks – a Germanic tribe from the lands between the Lower and Middle Rhine who entered Roman territory in the 3rd century AD. Later they settled in Gaul and considered themselves as the legitimate successors to the emperors of the Western Roman Empire.

Germani Corporis Custodes - the personal guard unit of the early Emperors (30 BCE – 68 AD) , composed of Germanic soldiers.

Gladius – the primary infantry sword of the late Republic and early Empire. It was a short stabbing sword based on similar swords used by the Celtiberians of Hispania.

Goths – Germanic peoples that included the Visigoths and Ostrogoths, originally from around Pomerania. Starting in the 3rd Century the Goths crossed the lower Danube and Black Sea to ravage the Balkans and Anatolia. By the 4th century they had spread into Western Europe.

Kontos or **Contus** – a long wooden cavalry lance, often used with two hands by heavy cavalry. Estimates put it at 12 feet long, which required the rider to direct the horse with his knees.

Laeti - a term used in the late Roman Empire to denote people from outside the Empire, permitted to settle on, and granted land in, imperial territory on condition that they had to provide recruits for the Roman military

Limitanei or **Ripenses** - literally meaning "the soldiers in frontier districts". After the reorganizations of the late 3rd and early 4th centuries, the limitanei garrisoned border fortifications and were not normally expected to fight far from their fortifications. The limitanei were lower-status and lower-paid than the comitatenses and palatini. The status distinction between scholae, palatini, comitatenses and limitanei had largely replaced the older distinction between praetorians, legionaries and auxiliaries. The limitanei and palatini both included legionary units among other kinds of troops. By the 6th and 7th centuries, the limitanei had become either part-time soldiers or unpaid militia.

Legio - the Legion of the Roman Army. By the late period the Legions had decreased in size from 5,000 to 1,000 men.

Limes - a line of frontier fortifications that bounded the border. At its height, the limes stretched from the North Sea outlet of the Rhine to near Regensburg on the Danube.

Isaurians – a people of Asia Minor centered on the Taurus Mountains. Isaurian marauders were fiercely independent mountain people who created havoc in neighboring districts under Macedonian and Roman occupations.

Lorica Hamata - a type of chain mail armor used by soldiers of the Roman Army. It was issued to both primary legionary and secondary auxiliary troops and was mostly manufactured out of bronze or iron. It comprised alternating rows of closed washer-like rings punched from iron sheets and rows of riveted rings made from drawn wire that ran horizontally, producing very flexible, reliable and strong armor.

Lorica Segmentata - a type of armor used by soldiers of the Roman Empire from the 1st century to the 3rd century, consisting of metal strips fastened to internal leather straps.

Lorica Squamata - a type of scale armor used by the Roman Army during different periods. It was made from small metal scales sewn to a fabric backing.

Marcomanni - a Germanic tribal confederation who eventually came to live in a powerful kingdom north of the Danube, somewhere near modern Bohemia, during the peak of power of the nearby Roman empire. According to Tacitus and Strabo they were Suebian.

Magister Militum - a top-level military command used in the late Roman Empire from the reign of Constantine onward. The title was given to the senior military officers in the East or West of the Empire.

Magister Officiorum - one of the most senior administrative officials in the late Roman Empire.

Milites - trained regular infantry of Rome.

Magister Militum Praesentalis - commander of one of the Imperial field armies.

Martiobarbuli – lead-weighted darts carried by infantrymen of the late Empire.

Notitia Dignitatum - a 14th century copy of a late Roman Document detailing the administrative organization of the Eastern and Western Empires, listing several thousand offices from the imperial court down to the provincial level, and individual army units. It is generally believed to represent the Western Roman Empire in the 410s and for the Eastern Roman Empire in the 390s.

Numerus - an infantry unit numbering around 640 men plus staff officers.

Optio - second in command of a century. The optio was stationed at the rear of the ranks to keep the troops in order. Their duties would include enforcing the orders of the centurion, taking over the centurion's command in battle should the need arise and supervising his subordinates, in addition to administration duties.

Orbiculi – circular decorative appliques added to late Roman clothing

Pagus - the smallest administrative district of a province.

Plumbata - see martiobarbuli.

Principate - (27 BC – 284 AD), the period of the Roman Empire that begins with Augustus in 27 BCE and ends in the 3rd century around 284 AD.

Praefectus - the formal title of many, fairly low to high-ranking, military or civil officials which was conferred by delegation from a higher authority.

Praefectus Castrorum - camp commandant

Praepositus - commander

Primus Pilus - the senior centurion of a Roman legion.

Princeps Protectorum - chief bodyguards

Primicerius - Roman equivalent to the modern lieutenant commander.

Privilegiis Scholarum - exemption of the Scholae Palatine from the recruiting tax

Protectores - elite guard unit of the late Roman Army

Pseudocomitatenses – a category of troops in the late Roman army. Although they were attached to a comitatus (higher-grade mobile armies), they enjoyed lower status and pay than the comitatenses. This is because their units had originally been classified as lower-grade limitanei ("border troops"), but at some point had been attached to a comitatus for a particular campaign and subsequently retained for long-term service.

Pteruges - protective leather or fabric strips worn around the waists of Roman and Greek warriors and soldiers.

Quadi were a Germanic tribe, about which little is definitively known. The only known information about them comes through reports from the Romans themselves.

Ridge helmet - a type of combat helmet used by soldiers of the late Roman army. It was characterized by the possession of a bowl made up of two or four parts, united by a longitudinal ridge.

Sarmatians - a large confederation of nomadic horsemen from the Iranian plains who were active from about the 5th century BCE to the 4th century AD, noted for their heavily armored, kontos bearing cavalry.

Schola Palatina - a mounted unit of Imperial Guards from the late Roman Empire.

Scutarii - shielded infantry

Scutum – the Latin word for shield.

Spangenhelm – a helmet of Germanic origin formed from metal strips that frame the helmet. The strips connect three to six steel or bronze plates. The frame takes a conical design that curves with the shape of the head and culminates in a point. The front of the helmet may include a nose protector.

Spatha - a straight sword between 30 and 39 inches long, used in the Roman Army from the 1st to 6th centuries AD. Later swords from the 7th to 10th centuries, like the Viking swords, are recognizable derivatives, and sometimes subsumed under the term spatha

Spiculum - a late Roman spear that replaced the pilum as the infantryman's main throwing javelin around 250 AD. Scholars suppose that it could have resulted from the gradual combination of the pilum and two German spears; the angon and the bebra. As more and more Germans joined the Roman army, their culture and traditions became a driving force for change. The spiculum was better than the old pilum when used as a thrusting spear, but still maintained some of the former weapon's penetrative power when thrown.

Symmachi – see Foederati

Tarantiarchia - a half Ala of approximately 256 men

Terrae Laeticae - land granted to laeti by the Imperial Administration to settle in the Empire.

Tesserarius - a watch commander in the Roman Army. There was one tesserarius to each century. They acted as seconds to the optiones.

Tribunus – commander of various kinds of military units

Turma – a Roman cavalry squadron. The turma was led by a decurio, who also led the first ten-strong file, while the other two files were led by subaltern officers (the successors of the early Empire's duplicarii and sesquiplicarii. Traces of this structure apparently survived in the 6th-century East Roman Army.

Vicarius – the administrative head of a diocese.

Velites – light infantry or skirmishers of the Republic. They rarely wore armor as they were the youngest and poorest soldiers in the legion and could not afford much equipment. They did carry small wooden shields for protection though, and wore a headdress made from wolf skin to allow officers to differentiate them and heavier legionaries.

Verutum - a short javelin used by velites for skirmishing to soften the enemy. The verutum's shaft was about 3.25 feet long.

Vexillatio - a temporarily detachment from a Legion during the Principate.

Fig 62. Dura Europos - Palmyra Gate (wikipedia)

Major Battles

Battle of Mediolanum (259) The Empire under Valerian was faced with attacks from the east and west. The Emperor made his son Gallienus co-emperor, in charge of the western borders against German tribes and internal enemies. Having subdued a rebellion in the Danube region, Gallienus was faced with a barbarian invasion along the Rhine and Danube from the Franks and Alemanni. Having drawn off troops from the frontier and around the capitol to defeat Ingenuus' rebellion in the Balkans, the border was thinly defended, as well as the area around Rome itself.

The Senate hastily armed the plebs and citizens of the un-walled city and presented a stiff defense to the invaders. The Alemanni retreated and were intercepted by Gallienus near Mediolanum with I Adiutrix, II Italica and II Parthica legions; during the battle huge numbers of Alemanni were killed. An outcome of this fighting was recognizing the need for more mobile forces, which began the transformation of the legions: Gallienus created a mobile field army with a great deal of cavalry.

Battle of Naissus (269 AD) was fought in present day Serbia by an alliance of Goths against an army led by the Emperor Claudius II, resulting in a Roman victory. The initial Goth incursion was a combined land-sea invasion that devastated the Balkans until the Emperor Gallienus subdued the Gothic leader Naulobatus in 267.

After the assassination of Gallienus and the ascension of Claudius II, an invasion of the Alemanni focused the Emperor's attention on the Rhine, which allowed a second Gothic sea invasion by a combination of tribes. They attacked several Black Sea settlements, as well as Byzantium, before entering the Aegean and ravaging the islands around Crete and Rhodes. The Goths were later defeated by the Roman Navy and had to retreat into the Balkan interior , where they were engaged by the Emperor near Naissus in 269.

The cavalry, under the command of Aurelian, deceived the Goths into thinking that they were retreating, but then turned back and charged. Large numbers of Goths were killed or captured; a numerous group escaped into Macedonia where they were pursued by the Romans who continued to harass them until they surrendered. The survivors were taken into the Roman army or allowed to settle within the Empire as a foederati. Although Claudius II is known as "Gothicus", the Goths continued to plague the Empire in the following decades.

Battle of Satala (298) This destroyed the Sassanid Persian army as an effective fighting force for several years. The Persian Shah, Narseh, declared war on Rome in 296 as part of the on-going border wars between the two Empires. The Persian forces initially invaded through Armenia, hoping to retake lands lost to the Armenian King Tiridates III with the peace of 287, then turned south into Roman Mesopotamia where they defeated a Roman Army under Galerius in what is now southern Turkey.

Through a combination of Persian inactivity and Roman reinforcement, Galerius was able to retake the offensive in 298 and pushed Narseh back into Armenia, whose terrain favored Roman infantry over Persian cavalry. Assisted by Armenian forces, Galerius won two overwhelming victories – the second being the destruction of the Sassanid army at Satala. Through stealth and local support, the Roman forces caught Narseh unprepared in his camp, capturing his treasury, wife and entourage.

Although the king escaped, Galerius was able to advance into the heart of Persia and captured the Sassanid capital at Ctesiphon. The Treaty of Nisibis ended the war and maintained peace until the 330's, when the military resurgence of Persia took place under Shapur II.

Battle of the Milvian Bridge (312) was the concluding battle of the civil conflict between the Emperors Constantine I and Maxentius on 28 October 312. Traditional Christian histories mark this as Constantine's conversion to Christianity – be it opportunistic or true faith – as Constantine's soldiers painted the Chi-Ro symbol on their shields. The arch that Constantine erected to this event, however, shows none of these symbols.

Both Constantine and Maxentius were sons of an Augustus who Diocletian had left in charge of the Empire in 306. While Constantine was accepted as an Augustus after his father's death, Maxentius was treated as a usurper and an uneasy truce was established between the eastern and western halves of the Empire. In the spring of 312, Constantine moved on Maxentius in Italy, winning battles at Turin and Verona. On 27 October, the opposing armies met outside Rome, with Maxentius defending the Milvian Bridge that crosses the Tiber, having the river at his back.

After defeating Maxentius cavalry with his own, Constantine launched an infantry attack which pushed Maxentius back. Hoping to make a stand in Rome, Maxentius' troops began to retreat across a temporary bridge that collapsed, leaving many units stranded, to be killed or taken prisoner. As a result of the battle, the Praetorian Guard was disbanded and replaced by the new Scholae Palatinae.

Battle of Samarra (June 363) was part of the invasion of Sassanid Persia by the Emperor Julian. While the outcome of the battle was inconclusive, the Emperor was mortally wounded in the battle. Julian hoped to replace Shah Shapur II with his brother Ormisdas, invading with a force of 65,000 soldiers. He initially split his forces, with 30,000 men under Procopius going into northern Mesopotamia and the other 35,000 under his own command marching south.

Julian won a victory outside the Persian capital of Ctesiphon, but Procopius did not reunite with him outside the capital. To make matters worse, he did not bring a proper siege train and was unable to take the capital with the forces available. Shapur devastated the area around Ctesiphon creating a supply issue for Julian and forcing him to retreat. Despite winning several skirmishes and a battle near Maranga, the Romans could not disengage and were running out of supplies.

To protect their lines from Persian cavalry, the army was moving in a giant square formation, which slowed down all movements. After three days without contact, the Persians attacked the rear guard, then the center and left wing. As Julian attempted to rally his forces, he became separated from his bodyguard and was hit in the back by a spear thrown from a Persian. Although the attack was repulsed, Julian died several hours later.

Jovian was proclaimed Emperor and continued the march to the Tigris, but unable to cross and in a dangerous situation, he signed a peace treaty with Shapur that ceded large areas of Mesopotamia, Georgia and Armenia, as well as several fortresses and cities.

Battle of Bagrevand (371) allowed the eastern Empire to recapture some of the lands lost several years earlier in Armenia, as a Romano-Armenian army defeated a Persian force under Shapur II. Shapur had convinced the Armenian King, Papas, to swear loyalty to him and prepared a large force to invade Armenia in 371. The Armenian leaders Mushegh Mamikonian and Movses Khorenatsi defeated the Persians and were able to reclaim lands ceded to the Persians by Jovian.

Battle of Adrianople (9 August 378), sometimes known as the Battle of Hadrianopolis, which resulted in a disastrous loss for the Eastern Roman army and indirectly hastened the fall of the western Roman Empire. An allied Gothic/Alan army led by Fritigern defeated the Romans, causing the death of the Emperor Valens. Invasions by the Huns in central Europe led to a wave of migrations from the Gothic tribes in 376, which were given permission to settle within the Empire as allies in exchange for military service and settlement. Abuses by local Roman commanders and administrators led to a revolt amongst the Goths under Fritigern.

The Eastern Emperor Valens sought help from the Western Emperor Gratian, who sent Frigeridus in command of reinforcements. This initiated a series of battles and skirmishes during which neither side gained the advantage. Trying to gain a numerical superiority, Valens pulled troops from Syria and Gratian sent more troops from Gaul. Valens took control of the forces in Thrace in 378, to deal directly with the Goths. The newly appointed local commander, Sebastianus, ambushed a small Gothic force near Adrianople, but this alerted Fritigern, who massed his troops at Nicopolis. When Gratian's troops finally arrived in the Balkans, they were harassed by the Alans and forced to retire. Valens did not want to miss out on a victory and decided to attack the Goths without waiting for reinforcements.

On 6 August, Valens had his troops make a reconnaissance of the Gothic camp, which seemed to hold 10,000 Goths marching toward Adrianople. This did not take into account a large force foraging to the north. Arriving at Adrianople, the Romans built a fortified camp and waited for the enemy. Valen's officers requested to postpone any action until the reinfocements could arrive from the west, but Valens wanted to strike as soon as possible, believing he had a numerically superior force.

Fritigern initially proposed an alliance in exchange for territory, but this was refused and on 9 August Valens marched his troops out of his camp towards the enemy encampment, located several hours march north from the city.

Fritigern wanted to delay any action until his detached cavalry could return. He burnt the fields around the hill where his fortified camp had been built, using smoke to harass the Roman troops. This further exacerbated the Romans, who already thought that they could obtain an easy victory into making a series of uncoordinated attacks on the Gothic line. By the time the attacking units were able to make headway, the returning Gothic cavalry routed the tired Roman heavy infantry and killed many troops along the line of retreat. The Emperor was killed along with other officers and his body was never found. The remaining Roman troops successfully defended the city of Adrianople. The army was crippled, but not destroyed by this battle; Theodosius I was later able to absorb the Goths as allies.

Battle of Thessalonica (380) Fritigern's Goths again defeated the reconstituted eastern Roman Army, this time under the command of Theodoius I. Theodosius retreated to Thessalonica and surrendered control of operations to the Western Emperor, Gratian.

Battle of the Frigidus, also called the **Battle of the Frigid River, (5–6 September 394)** was a battle between the Eastern army under Theodosius and the Western army under Eugenius. Theodosius' defeat of Eugenius consolidated rule of the Empire back under one Emperor for the last time. This battle is often seen as the last gasp of the pagans versus Christianity. When the Western Emperor Valentinian II, borther-in-law of Theodosius, was found dead in May 392, it was rumored that he had been murdered. The magister militum, Arbogast, elevated the magister scrinii, Flavius Eugenius, as Emperor, who was an acceptable candidate to the Senate and people of Rome.

When Eugenius supported restoring pagan shrines, he ran into conflict with the Bishop of Milan and Theodosius. In addition, Eugenius removed all civil administrators who Theodosius had appointed, without consulting the Eastern Emperor. By January 393, Theodosius decided to proclaim his son, Honorius, as western Augustus and invaded the west.

The armies met somewhere in modern Slovenia, with Eugenia and his Magister setting up a statue of Jupiter on the edge of the battlefield. Theodosius initially charged the western forces with little or no reconnaissance, resulting in heavy casualties and the western forces holding the field. Arbogast attempted to seal the rear of Theodosius' forces to cut off possible retreat, but his men went over to the Eastern Emperor.

Theodosius attacked once again, but this time he was aided by a heavy wind storm which blew clouds of dust in the faces of the defenders, and supposedly blew their arrows back at them. Eugenius was captured and beheaded, while Arbogast managed to escape only to commit suicide. The Empire was united again under one great leader, but he died four months later and left the Empire divided again between his young children, Honorius and Arcadius. More importantly, some historians have argued that this battle caused human losses which could not easily be replaced, weakening the Roman ability to defend the borders of the Empire and obliging them to rely more heavily on the foederati.

Battle of Faesulae (406) fought during the Gothic invasion of the Empire in the early 5th century. After repelling Goths at Pollentia and Verona, Stilicho moved to counter raids by Vandals and Goths under Radagaisus around modern day Florence. Gathering support from Goth and Hun allies, Stilicho defeated the invaders at Faesulae and executed Radagaisus. Survivors fled to join the forces of Alaric.

Sack of Rome (410) While Rome was no longer the capital of the Empire since 402, it still represented the glory of the Empire and its sack for the first time since 387 BCE had major reverberations in Europe.

At the death of Fritigern, Alaric was chosen as the leader of the Visigoths in the early 390's. He started moving outside of the designated Gothic areas and raiding parts of the Eastern Roman Empire, until he was defeated by Theodosius and Stilicho in 392. In 394 Alaric commanded a contingent of Theodosius' army at the battle of Frigidus. As a result he was granted the title of comes, but during the battle the Roman generals had made the Goths take on the brunt of the initial fighting and thus Alaric thought that he should have been rewarded with a higher office.

When Theodosius died in 395, the Visigoths considered their treaty with Rome as a personal one and abrogated it, raiding the Danubian provinces. Theodosius' sons were still minors and both under the nominal control of Stilicho, even though Rufinus was the praetorian prefect of the East and controlled Constantinople. Rufinus promised Alaric lands in Greece and he withdrew from Constantinople. Although Stilicho had Alaric surrounded on several occasions, he did not destroy the Visigoths. Alaric was eventually given the title of magister militum of Illyricum. He was later stripped of this title by the new praetorian prefect Aurelianus in 400. A large number of Goths were massacred in Constantinople shortly thereafter and, fearing his position, Alaric moved on to Italy while Stilicho was defending the frontier against Vandals and Alans.

Stilicho returned with foederati and pushed the Goths back, but the Emperor Honorius feared the attacks and moved the capitol to the more easily defendable Ravenna. Over the next few years Alaric reconciled with Stilicho, but court intrigue resulted in the death of Stilicho and the payment of tribute to the Goths. Alaric invaded Italy again and laid siege to Rome, starting in 408. Eventually the city agreed to pay a large ransom and Alaric left in December 408. Through treachery and bad leadership, Alaric laid siege to Rome again in 409 and finally in 410. Outraged by an assassination attempt, his troops entered Rome on 24 August through a trick and pillaged the city for three days.

Battle of Ravenna also known as the **Battle of Rimini** (432) was part of the continuous civil conflict in the western Empire, this time between the junior magister militum, Flavius Aetius, and the senior magister militum Bonifacius. Although Bonifacius' forces were victorious, he died from his wounds several months later, being succeeded by his son Sebastian. Aetius was forced to flee, but allied with the Huns and was later able to defeat Sebastian and become de facto ruler of the west.

Siege of Narbonne (436-7) The Visigothic foederati of Aquitania were raiding in Gaul and had laid siege to the city of Narbonne in late 436. The Roman general Litorius was able to concentrate a force drawn from the Gallic Field Army and Hun auxiliaries in order to attack the Visigoths before they could organize battle lines and routed them.

Battle of the Catalaunian Plains (or Fields), also called the **Battle of Châlons** or the **Battle of Maurica (451)** The Huns under Attila invaded western Europe through Gaul in 450, destroying several cities until they were stopped outside of Châlons by a combined force of Romans under the magister utriusque militiae Flavius Aetius and the Visigoth King Theodoric I.

 The Huns were besieging the city and about to affect a breach in the city walls when the Romano-Gothic force arrived. The battle took place on a large ridge. The Huns seized the right side of the ridge, while the Romans seized the left, with the unoccupied crest between the two armies. The allied line was made up of Visigoths on the right side, the Romans on the left, and other allied tribes in the middle. The Huns attempted to take the ridge, but were pushed back by the Romans under Aetius and the Gothic left flank under Thorismund. Theodoric was killed while leading an attack against rival western Goths, who were allied to the Huns. The Visigoths pushed past the Huns' wagon laager and forced Attila to seek safety within it. The next day the armies faced each other at a distance, with the Huns eventually retreating during the night. Aetius convinced Theodoric's son, Thorismund, to return to his capital of Tolosa, to claim the Kingship before his brothers could.

The Sack of Rome (455) This was the second of the three sacks imposed on the citizens of Rome over the last century of the Empire. The death of Valentinian III and the ascension of Petronius Maximus disrupted the dynastic plans of the Vandal King, Genseric. His son was previously betrothed to Valentinian's daughter, but at the death of the Emperor in 455 Petronius Maximus married her to his son. Genseric viewed this as voiding the peace treaty with Rome and attacked the city.

 The Vandals knocked down the aqueducts as they approached Rome, but agreed not to destroy the city if its doors were open to them. Petronius Maximus fled rather than fight. The Vandals looted a large amount of treasure over the course of fourteen days. In addition to the loot, Genseric took Valentinian's wife and daughter as hostages, and eventually married his son Huneric to Eudocia.

Battle of Agrigentum (456) took place in Sicily near modern Agrigento, where Western Roman troops under Ricimer defeated Vandals under Genseric. The Vandals had sacked Rome in 455 and subsequently raided through Spain on their way to conquering North Africa. To counter Vandal threats to the western Mediterranean, Ricimer landed troops in Sicily which was composed of marines, auxiliaries and foederati.

 The Romans set up a defensive position in a forested area, repelling repeated attacks by the Vandals until they were finally able to drive off the enemy force. Those Vandals who survived sailed north to Corsica, where they were finally defeated by Ricimer in a sea battle. Upon returning to Rome, Ricimer, along with Majorian and Aegidus, seized power from the Western Emperor Avitus and proclaimed Majorian Emperor.

Battle of Orléans (463) stalled the Gothic invasion of Gaul as the western forces under the magister militum Aegidus defeated the Visigoths under Theodoric II and his brother Federico. Aegidus had been initial removed from his position by Ricimer, after the assassination of the Emperor Majorian in 461, which resulted in the proclaimation of Flavius Severus Serpentius as new Emperor. This was not accepted by several provinces and by the Eastern Emperor, allowing Aegidus to retain support in Gaul.

Ricimer encouraged the Goths to attack in Gaul, to distract their attention from Italy, but Aegidius was able to mass a large force and rout the Visigoths near Orléans, resulting in the death of Federico.

Battle of Déols (470) an army of Bretons under Riothamus were defeated by the Visigoths in northern Gaul.

The Battle of Ravenna (476) is traditionally considered one of the last battles of the western Roman Empire, taking place on 2 September 476, between King Odoacer of the Heruli and the remnants of the Roman Army. Even though the Heruli were foederati, they demanded a third of Italy for their control due to the chaotic nature of the Empire at that time. When this was refused by Orestes, the commanding general of the west and father of the nominal Emperor Romulus Augustulus, Odoacer led troops in revolt, pillaging Pavia and executing Orestes.

The Roman garrison of Ravenna was defeated by the foederati and the city was captured along with the Emperor. Romulus Augustulus abdicated and the imperial insignia was sent to Constantinople.

Sources
Select Bibliography

Barker P., Heath I., *The Armies and Enemies of Imperial Rome*, Wargames Research Group, 1981

Bishop M. C., Coulston J. C., *Roman Military Equipment From the Punic Wars to the Fall of Rome*, Oxbow Books, 2006

Brzezinski R., Mielczarek M., Embleton G., *The Sarmatians 600 BC-AD 450*, Osprey Publishing, 2002

Connolly P., *Greece and Rome at War*, Macdonald Phoebus Ltd, 1981

Cowan R., McBride A., *Imperial Roman Legionary AD 161-284*, Osprey Publishing, 2003

Cowan R., O'Brogain S., *Roman Guardsman 62 BC-AD 324*, Osprey Publishing, 2014

Cowan R., O'Brogain S., *Roman Legionary AD 284-337*, Osprey Publishing, 2014

D'Amato R., Sumner G., *Roman Military Clothing (3): AD 400-640*, Osprey Publishing, 2005

Duncan-Jones, Richard, *Structure and Scale in the Roman Economy*, Cambridge University Press, 2002

Elliot P., *Legions in Crisis: Transformation of the Roman Soldier AD 192-284*, Fonthill Media, 2014

Elton H., *Warfare in Roman Europe AD 350-425*, Clarendon Press, 1998

Goldsworthy A., *The Fall of the West: The Slow Death of the Roman Superpower*, Weidenfeld & Nicolson, 2009

Macdowall S., Embleton G., *Late Roman infantryman 236-565 AD*, Osprey Publishing, 1994

Macdowall S., Hook C., *Late Roman cavalryman 236-565 AD*, Osprey Publishing, 1995

Macdowall S., McBride A., *Germanic Warrior AD 236-568*, Osprey Publishing, 1996

Nicasie M., *Twilight of Empire: The Roman Army from the Reign of Diocletian until the Battle of Adrianople*, Brill Academic Publishers, 1998

Nicolle D., McBride A., *Arthur and the Anglo-Saxon Wars*, Osprey Publishing, 1984

Nicolle D., McBride A., *Romano-Byzantine Armies 4th-9th centuries*, Osprey Publishing, 1992

Nicolle D., McBride A., *Rome's Enemies 5: the Desert Frontier*, Osprey Publishing, 1991

Rankow B., Hook R., *The Praetorian Guard*, Osprey Publishing, 1994

Simkins M., Embleton R., *The Roman Army from Hadrian to Constantine*, Osprey Publishing, 1979

Sumner G., *Roman Military Clothing (1): 100 BC-AD 200*, Osprey Publishing, 2002

Sumner G., Roman *Military Clothing (2): AD 200-400*, Osprey Publishing, 2003

Travis J., Travis H., *Roman Body Armour,* Amberley, 2012

Travis J., Travis H., *Roman Helmets*, Amberley, 2015

Travis J., Travis H., *Roman Shields*, Amberley, 2014

Treadgold, Warren, *Byzantium and Its Army 284 - 1081.* Stanford University Press, 1995

Wilcox P., Embleton G., *Rome's Enemies 1: Germanics and Dacians*, Osprey Publishing, 1982

Sitography

The following web pages, taken from Wikipedia, were particularly useful during the researches for the present book; they contain much of the same basic information included in my text and are a reliable source for a first approach to the relative topics.

https://en.wikipedia.org/wiki/Late_Roman_army
https://en.wikipedia.org/wiki/Timeline_of_the_Roman_Empire

https://en.wikipedia.org/wiki/Auxilia_palatina
https://en.wikipedia.org/wiki/Scholae_Palatinae
https://en.wikipedia.org/wiki/Excubitors
https://en.wikipedia.org/wiki/Protectores_Augusti_Nostri
https://en.wikipedia.org/wiki/Domesticus_(Roman_Empire)
https://en.wikipedia.org/wiki/Imperial_German_Bodyguard
https://en.wikipedia.org/wiki/Laeti
https://en.wikipedia.org/wiki/Equites_Stablesiani
https://en.wikipedia.org/wiki/Equites_Dalmatae
https://en.wikipedia.org/wiki/Battle_of_Adrianople
https://en.wikipedia.org/wiki/Bagaudae
https://en.wikipedia.org/wiki/Clothing_in_ancient_Rome#Roman_clothing_of_Late_Antiquity_.28after_284_AD.29
https://en.wikipedia.org/wiki/Late_Roman_ridge_helmet
https://en.wikipedia.org/wiki/Spangenhelm
https://en.wikipedia.org/wiki/Lorica_segmentata
https://en.wikipedia.org/wiki/Lorica_hamata
https://en.wikipedia.org/wiki/Lorica_squamata
https://en.wikipedia.org/wiki/Muscle_cuirass
https://en.wikipedia.org/wiki/Scutum_(shield)
https://en.wikipedia.org/wiki/Spatha
https://en.wikipedia.org/wiki/Spiculum
https://en.wikipedia.org/wiki/Angon
https://en.wikipedia.org/wiki/Verutum
https://en.wikipedia.org/wiki/Plumbata
https://en.wikipedia.org/wiki/Kontos_(weapon)
https://en.wikipedia.org/wiki/Sagittarii
https://en.wikipedia.org/wiki/Composite_bow
https://en.wikipedia.org/wiki/Sling_(weapon)#Staff_sling
https://en.wikipedia.org/wiki/Auxilia#Archers
https://en.wikipedia.org/wiki/Vandals
https://en.wikipedia.org/wiki/Huns
https://en.wikipedia.org/wiki/Palmyra

List of Maps and Illustrations

Look for more books from Winged Hussar Publishing, LLC – E-books, paperbacks and Limited Edition hardcovers. The best in history, science fiction and fantasy at:

https://wingedhussarpublishing.com

or follow us on Facebook at:

Winged Hussar Publishing LLC

Or on twitter at:

WingHusPubLLC

For information and upcoming publications

Look for these other military history books from Winged Hussar Publishing

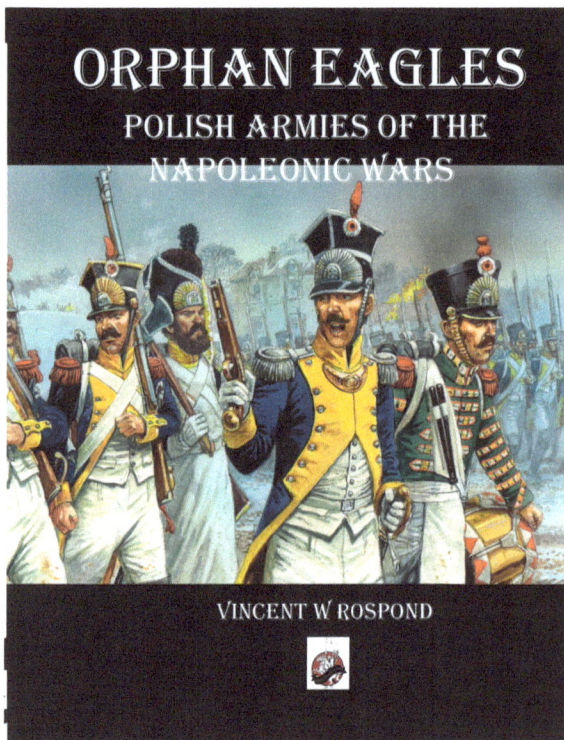

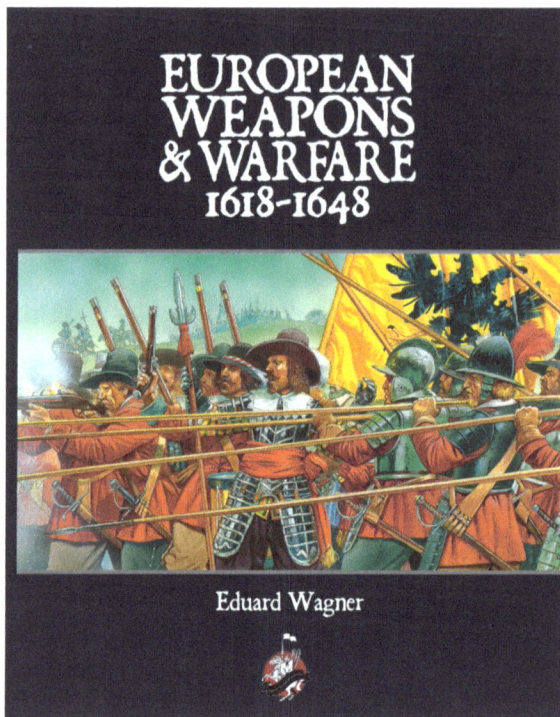

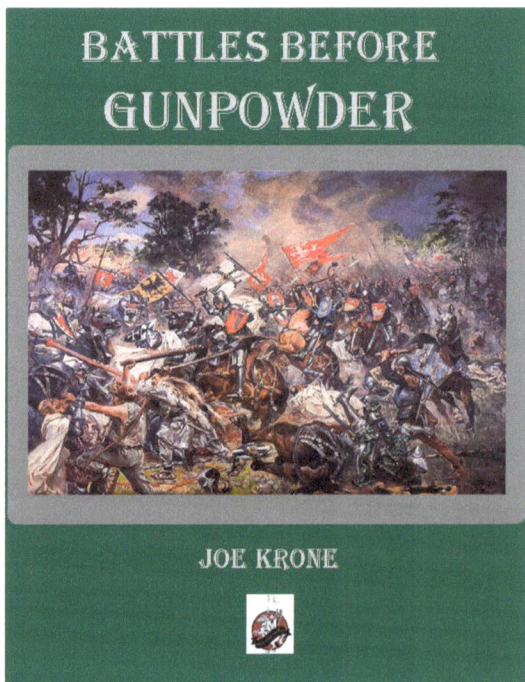

ORPHAN EAGLES
POLISH ARMIES OF THE
NAPOLEONIC WARS

VINCENT W ROSPOND

EUROPEAN WEAPONS & WARFARE 1618-1648

Eduard Wagner

BATTLES BEFORE GUNPOWDER

JOE KRONE

THE RUSSIAN IMPERIAL CAVALRY IN 1914

BY VLADIMIR A. EMMANUEL

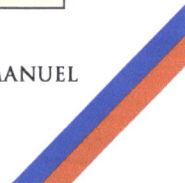

Index

About the Author

Gabriele Esposito is a researcher and expert on military history, specialized in uniformology. He works as a freelance author for the major publishing houses of this sector, including Osprey Publishing, Helion & Company, Winged Hussar Publishing and Partizan Press. Mr. Esposito is the author of various books and essays on military subject; in addition, he is a regular contributor to many magazines covering military history: *Ancient Warfare Magazine, Medieval Warfare Magazine, Classic Arms & Militaria Magazine, Guerres et Histoire, History of War* and *Focus Storia*. His interests and expertise range from the Sumerians to the modern post-colonial conflicts, but his main field of research is the military history of Latin America, especially in the 19th century. He is among the leading authorities on South American uniformology.

About the Artist

Giuseppe Rava is one of the leading military artists in the world, working for some of the most important magazines and publishing houses of this area, both in Europe and the USA. His stunning works of art are famous around the world for their incredibly vivid style and great accuracy in the rendition of the smaller details. During his artistic career, Giuseppe has represented soldiers and battles from every period of history and from every corner of the world, remaining always true to his own original style but at the same time exploring new artistic horizons. Entirely self-taught, he has established himself as the heir of some of the most important military illustrators of the past, like Detaille, Meissonier and Angus McBride. His imaginative use of colours and lights has brought thousands of warriors and soldiers to life again.